SHE

The King

RISE OF LOKMATA AHILYABAI HOLKAR

SHE

The King

RISE OF LOKMATA AHILYABAI HOLKAR

Aditi Narayani

YATRA BOOKS
An imprint of Vani Prakashan Group

vaniprakashan.com

Hardback First Edition : 2025

Yatra Books is an imprint of Vani Prakashan Group

Head Office

4695, 21-A, Daryaganj, New Delhi 110 002, India
Phone : +91 11 23273167, 23275710

— Registered Bookstores and Offices —

Ashok Rajpath, Patna-800 004, Bihar
Coffee House Campus, Mahatma Gandhi Marg, Prayagraj-211 001, Uttar Pradesh
Mahatma Gandhi Antarrashtriya Hindi Vishwavidyalaya, Wardha-442 001, Maharashtra

sales@vaniprakashan.in
vaniprakashan@gmail.com

She : The King
Rise of Lok Mata Ahilyabai Holkar
by Aditi Narayani

ISBN : 978-93-48235-75-6
Biography/History

Price : ₹ 400

Printed and bound in India at City Press, Delhi-110095

This book is dedicated to women from the margins for their strength and resilience in face of struggle.

Preface

As I reflect on my journey to write this book about Lok Mata Ahilyabai Holkar, I am reminded of a conversation with my Guru, a renowned social activist and thinker, during the summer of 2023. He mentioned Ahilyabai, and I, in my ignorance, thought of her as merely a queen who built temples. Little did I know that this brief introduction would set me on a path of discovery, leading me to be deeply inspired by her remarkable life and legacy. Today, as I pen these words, I am filled with a sense of awe and reverence for this extraordinary woman.

My research for the book took me to Chondi, the humble village in Maharashtra where Ahilyabai was born. The aura of that place left me awestruck, as if the very essence of her spirit still resonates there. It was as if the land itself whispered stories of her courage, wisdom, and compassion. Ahilyabai Holkar was more than just a philanthropist who built temples; she was a visionary leader, a patron of the arts and culture, and a champion of women empowerment and social harmony. Her reign in Malwa, marked by wisdom and inclusivity, became a model for effective governance. She transformed Indore from a village to a thriving city, fostering an environment where artforms flourished alongside industries. Her contributions to Indian architecture are legendary, with numerous temples, ghats, and dharmshalas across the country standing as testaments to her service and generosity. Her legacy further extends to her efforts in promoting social welfare, empowering marginalized communities, and nurturing a sense of cultural unity. This book is a heartfelt tribute to Punyashlok Queen Ahilyabai Holkar, whose life has inspired me to see the world through her eyes— eyes that saw beauty in resilience, strength in compassion, and unity in diversity.

Through these pages, I hope to share her story with you, not merely as a figure of history, but as someone who embodies courage, wisdom, and astute leadership. As we delve into her life, let us remember that her legacy is not just about the past; it is a blueprint for our future— a reminder that true leadership is about serving others, fostering harmony, and leaving the world a better place than we found it.

I am deeply grateful to my parents, Dr. Sanjay Paswan and Dr. Pramanshi Jaideva for their constant words of guidance and encouragement and for being my pillars of strength. Your dedication to education and your belief in my potential has inspired me every step of the way. There are no words to describe how indebted I am to my dear husband, Raj Singh, his unwavering support, and patience have been invaluable in shaping me into the person I am today. I am grateful to my principal Prof Pratyush Vatsala, Lakshmibai College, University of Delhi for her unwavering support. I am deeply indebted to Aditi Maheshwari Didi, my publisher, for her invaluable inputs and unwavering care, which have been instrumental in making this book possible. Your love and support mean the world to me, and I look forward to sharing this accomplishment with you. Special mention to my lovely students, Sanjana Sinha and Devanshi Mehta for helping me to navigate through the book. Your enthusiasm and curiosity have reminded me of the joy of teaching and learning. I am proud to see you both grow, and your encouragement has fueled my passion for this project.

"This book is based on secondary sources available and draws heavily on the research and insights of numerous scholars and authors, whose contributions are deeply appreciated and acknowledged".

With gratitude and appreciation.

Prologue

Today, as we celebrate the tri-centenary birth anniversary of the Maratha Queen Lok Mata Ahilya Bai Holkar – administrator par excellence and a visionary with spiritual inclination. A woman who left an indelible mark on Indian history and has compelled us to question the androcentric nature of writing of history. She was not only a queen who has defined the ethos of being a true king with her administrative skills, military strength and diplomatic skills but also laid the foundation of what empowerment means to us, the women of the 21st century. In the fight for our rights, we often forget our duties, duties towards our family, and duties towards the nation. Her life exemplifies a perfect balance between the inner and outer world.

The title of the book is special and close to my heart, as we have read only about the kings who have made their presence marked in nation building and have often times forgotten and obliterated the contributions of queens who were equally involved in the evolution of Bharat. We always see a queen in relation to a king, who is a keeper of *Raja-Dharma*, who shoulders the responsibilities of state and his people, while an able queen plays a supportive role, by his side. Lokmata Ahilyabai had everything a queen is supposed to portray, at the same time she also did everything a King, in an hour of need, must perform to keep his people and kingdom safe.

We will also learn later how she transformed herself from a daughter to an able queen, to eventually becoming a great ruler – She the King.

Ahilya's rise to power questions this dominant heteronormative understanding of history writing wherein a widowed woman took care of her people for 30 years guided by her innate generosity and principles rooted in Bhartiya civilizational ethos and yet does not find the space she deserves in history books. Thirty years is a significant time, especially during the period of major upheaval of first half of 18th century with the Mughal empire breaking up and no single power center left, and with the East India Company setting up its bases and gaining regional power. This was also a period when Marathas were on a rise. A time of several wars, where battles were being fought across the subcontinent, and kings were engaged in finding recourses in either treaties or treachery in order to gain new grounds, hold position and concentrate power. Amidst all this we find fierce ruler Queen Ahilya Bai Holkar, who unfortunately remains absent in history books.

Even though historians write of her 'tolerance' of people of different faiths and beliefs, but little is written about how Lokmata not only reconsecrated temples but also built mosques to promote intercommunal harmony during her reign. Ahilya Bai truly celebrated all her subjects. Ahilya Bai is believed to be the great ruler that she was due to her undying faith in Hinduism. She regularly attended Purana recitals and yagnas, believing that the spiritually charged environment would help her stand firm on her principles. It was her immersion in the philosophy of Hinduism that eventually led to a monumental change in the architectural expression of the faith. Ahilya Bai reconsecrated the *Jyotirlingas* across the country as a tribute to Lord Shiva. Renovations in Somnath, Varanasi, Trambak, Gaya, Pushkar, Vrindavan, Nathdwar, Haridwar, Badrinath, Kedarnath and many other sacred sites were undertaken during her reign. To defend against attacks and iconoclasm, she came up with the idea of installing the idols in secret shrines under the temples, providing an additional layer of security. Ahilya Bai's tireless attempts to resurrect these temples were, on one hand, an act of defiance against Mughal autocracy and, on the other, bound her subjects together, with the thread of civilizational ethos, independent of their social-religious identity.

The beautiful Maheshwari saris that we wear today are also part of the queen's legacy. She not only promoted the traditional weave but also paved the way for skilling women, thus empowering them. The production of these saris was not only a way to increase the revenue collection of the state but provided a steady source of income to the weavers. Under her encouragement, the production of Maheswari saris gained momentum and popularity. Today, their production remains alive as a traditional craft of Maharashtra. Ahilya Bai also made efforts to develop the city of Indore, conserve forests and animals, and promote trade and commerce in her kingdom.

If true Ram Rajya was attained by any ruler, it was under Ahilya Bai's graceful reign where farmers flourished, faiths were restored, and inclusivity found its rightful place. Her efforts in mainstreaming the Bhil and Gond castes are less talked about but remain an important achievement. She commanded respect not just from her contemporaries but from historians and intellectuals that came later with the likes of Jadunath Sarkar, Annie Besant and John Keay. It is a travesty that Ahilya Bai Holkar is not nearly as celebrated nationally as she is regionally. Her localization reveals how the rest of the nation conveniently forgets a woman of her stature due to gender bias. Ahilya Bai's rule serves as an example of inclusive policymaking. She worked to develop her state and uplift her subjects on various levels. Her legacy is not only remembered for her administrative acumen but also for paving the way for future generations of the Holkar dynasty towards effective governance that transcends gender norms. To bind her legacy only to her contribution to temple renovation would also be unjust. In assessing her impact, it is impossible to overlook her overall governance, which helped bring Samajik Samrasta (social harmony) in the truest sense and provided a blueprint for what Ram Rajya in today's era would look like.[1]

1 Paswan, A. N. (2024, December 23). *When a Holkar queen gave India Ram Rajya.* The Indian Express. Retrieved April 7, 2025, from https://indianexpress.com/article/opinion/columns/when-a-holkar-queen-gave-india-ram-rajya-9362764/

भारतीय उच्च अध्ययन संस्थान
राष्ट्रपति निवास, शिमला- 171005 दूरभाष: कार्यालय +91-177-2830006 फैक्स +91-177-2831389
INDIAN INSTITUTE OF ADVANCED STUDY
RASHTRAPATI NIWAS, SHIMLA -171005
Phones : Office : +91-177-2830006 Fax : +91-177-2831389
e-mail: chairperson@iias.co.in; prof.shashinrabha@gmail.com

Professor ShashiPrabha Kumar
Chairperson

FOREWORD

It gives me immense pleasure to write these words about the remarkable book in hand, very ably authored by Aditi Paswan on the life and legacy of Lokmata Ahilya Bai Holkar. The book is suitably titled as follows:

AHILYA BAI HOLKAR
She - The King
Rise of LokMata Ahilyabai Holkar

Currently we are celebrating the 300th birth anniversary of the great Indian Queen Ahilya Bai Holkar who ruled over the Malwa region for three decades. It is therefore heartening to note that several books are being written about her multi-faceted personality and enormous contribution for empowering the women of our country. Born in an ordinary family herself, she rose to become an extraordinary person with an innate vision for social justice and a matching mission for accomplishing her aim.

Author of the book deserves plaudits for her painstaking effort in making the book readable as well as reliable.

I am sure that the present volume will not only offer valuable information about the dynamic reign of Ahilya Bai Holkar but will also provide fresh insights into the onward journey of Indian women through the last three centuries.

Hope that the book will be widely read and duly appreciated.

With best wishes

SKumar 2/4/25

Prof. Dr. ShashiPrabha Kumar
Chairperson
Indian Institute of Advanced Study,
Shimla-171005

श्रीमंत सरकार उदयसिंह प्रतापसिंह राव होळकर

होळकर वाड़ा, 12 पंढरीनाथ मार्ग,
इन्दौर (म.प्र.) 452 004
मो. 8305123452

क्रमांक

दिनांक 05/01/2025

Dear Dr Aditi Paswan,

Thank you for letting us know that you are working on Punyashloka Lokmata Ahilyabai Holkar. She has been a symbol of Indian culture, religion, spirituality, modernisation, and women empowerment.

Her contribution is remembered by the world for over 300 years. As you have shown sincere interest in her legacy, we are glad to support you with the archival materials. Your book, *She : The King-Rise of Lokamata Ahilya Bai Holkar,* to be published by Vani Prakashan, will hopefully attract young and serious scholars, general readers, and fellow researchers.

Wish you all the best for your future endeavors.

Holkar

Shrimant Sardar Udaysingh Pratapsingh Rao Holkar

Contents

CHAPTER - 1

A Journey Begins: Early Life and Marriage

Born in 1725 to a shepherd (Dhangar/Gadariya)[1] family in what is today Maharashtra's Ahilya Nagar[2] district Ahilya Bai Holkar rose to become a visionary ruler for the masses, who preserved and encouraged India's spiritual integrity and displayed administrative ingenuity and political impartiality. Her exceptional leadership skills were evident in the 30 years of peace and financial stability that her kingdom experienced during her reign. When we talk about women's empowerment, we often overlook figures from our own history, the brave daughters who contributed towards building the India we see today. The historical glorification of men and their deeds hides the stories of countless women who served their nation. Perhaps this is why Ahilya Bai found little mention in national rhetoric.[3]

1 The Dhangar (also known as Gadariya in some regions) are a traditionally pastoral community in India. They are primarily involved in sheep and goat herding, farming, and other agrarian activities. Their name is derived from the Sanskrit word 'Dhenu' (meaning cow) and 'Gar' (meaning protection), indicating their historical role as cattle herders.

2 Ahmednagar was officially renamed Ahilya Nagar on October 4, 2024, following a decision by the Maharashtra Cabinet. The name changes honor the legacy of Ahilyabai Holkar, an influential 18th century queen of the Maratha Empire, who was born in Chondi village within the Ahmednagar district. The announcement of the renaming was first made by Maharashtra Chief Minister Eknath Shinde on 31st May 31, 2023, coinciding with Ahilyabai Holkar's 298th birth anniversary.

3 Paswan, A. N. (2024, December 23). When a Holkar queen gave India Ram Rajya. The Indian Express. Retrieved April 7, 2025, from https://indianexpress.com/article/opinion/columns/when-a-holkar-queen-gave-india-ram-rajya-9362764/

Manakoji Shinde, Ahilyabai's father and the Patil of Chondi, was a man of strong moral values, while her mother, Sushilabai, embodied the virtues of righteousness and balance, seamlessly managing household responsibilities with grace.[4] From an early age, Ahilyabai displayed exceptional intelligence and an eagerness to learn, laying the foundation for a remarkable future. Her parents not only ensured she was well-versed in reading, writing, and religious scriptures but also instilled in her practical wisdom through puranic tales. She engaged in pursuits uncommon for women of her time— military training, horse riding, and archery— skills that would later define her leadership and courage. With a steadfast focus and an unwavering spirit, she emerged as a visionary, setting the stage for a legacy that would shape the cultural and political landscape of India.

John Malcolm sums up her character and said that, "*It is an extraordinary picture, a female without vanity, a bigot without intolerance, a mind imbued with the deepest superstition, yet receiving no impression except what prompted the happiness of those under its influence, a being exercising, in the most active and able manner, despotic power not merely with sincere humility, but under the severest moral restraint that a strict conscience could impose on human action and all this combined with the greatest indulgence for the weakness and faults of others. Such at least is the account which the natives of Malwa give Ahilya Bai, with whom her name is stained, and she is styled an "avatar or incarnation of the Divinity"*.[5]

4 Thakur V Vasudeo, Life and Life's work of Shree Devi Ahilya Bai Holkar , Holkar state History, printed by C.M, Shah Modern Printery Limited, Indore available on https://archive.org/details/in.ernet.dli.2015.199825/page/n5/mode/2up?view=theater accessed on September 26,2024.

5 John Malcolm, A Memoir of Central India, Vol. I (London: Kingsbury, Parbury, and Allen, 1823).

Despite being born as a Shudra,[6] her revered legacy continues to inspire women across the generations. She belonged to the Dhangar community, a shepherd community which lives in various states including Maharashtra, Gujarat, Karnataka, and Andhra Pradesh. The Dhangars, known by names such as Golla and Kuruba in other regions, are part of Maharashtra's Vimukta Jati and Nomadic Tribes (VJNT), though they have long sought recognition as a Scheduled Tribe (ST).[7] While their exact population is uncertain due to the lack of data, it is believed that the Dhangar community constitutes about 9% of Maharashtra's population, which amounts to nearly one crore people[8]. The Dhangar community is traditionally associated with both nomadic and semi-nomadic pastoral lifestyles, as well as agrarian practices in rural areas. They follow indigenous folk traditions and worship deities such as Khandoba, Biroba, Pandurang, Jyotiba, Banubai, Mahalsa, Tulja Bhavani, and Mandhardevi. Despite her birth in a marginalized community, Ahilyabai's exceptional leadership transcended her background, breaking the norms of her time and demonstrating that greatness is not bound by social origin.[9]

According to, D. D. Kosambi in his book titled "Living Prehistory in India," writes, "*another primitive group in the Deccan-the Dhangars-are a caste rather than a tribe. Some*

6 The term "Shudras" refers to one of the four varnas (social classes) in the traditional Hindu Varna system. Shudras are typically associated with occupations related to service and labor, such as artisans, craftsmen, and agricultural workers. She was born in Dhangar Community who were traditionally Shepherds.

7 Parthasarathi Biswas, Indian Express, 2024, August 23, https://indianexpress.com/article/explained/dhangars-maharashtra-elections-caste-9524048/

8 Anand Kshirsagar: https://indianexpress.com/article/opinion/columns/maharashtra-dhangar-community-caste-census-9267965/ accessed on 26th October 2025.

9 Parthasarathi Biswas, Indian Express, 2024, August 23, https://indianexpress.com/article/explained/dhangars-maharashtra-elections-caste-9524048/

of them are farmers; others specialize in the manufacture of woolen blankets. At least one Dhangar family, the Holkars, took up military life early in the 18th century and rose to princely status as the maharajas of Indore. Today the members of one Dhangar group follow tribal ways and earn a living as itinerant herdsmen. Each Dhangar band numbers about 12 people. Leading a flock of perhaps 300 sheep, the band spends the eight dry months of the year in a round of travel that rarely covers less than 200 miles and may range as far as 400 miles"[10].

The Making of a Queen: Rise to Power

Ahilya's journey in becoming a transformative ruler began the day she was born. A Shiva devotee, Ahilya Bai Holkar with her mother used to worship every morning at the temple where Bajirao Peshwa and his commander, Malhar Rao Holkar first saw Ahilya. She radiated the aura of devotion, strength, and simplicity. Ahilya's personality sparked a clear vision in Malhar Rao's eye about the future of his kingdom. He knew that she would be the key to a transformative future of his family and his kingdom.

For Khande Rao, his son (with Gautamabai), was a concern for him then as he struggled to complete his education and master the martial arts, leaving him unprepared for the responsibilities of leadership.[11] Malhar Rao considered Ahilya's virtues of dedication, wisdom, and integrity as a source that could bring change in his son. Malhar Rao was of a belief that Ahilya would be a suitable partner for Khande

10 Kosambi D. D (2013)., Living Prehistory in India (New Delhi: Vikas Publishing House,).

11 Joshi, Govindram Keshavram (1978) Ahilyabai Holkar (Jivan Charitra), provides a Hindi biography of Ahilyabai.

Rao who will instill in him the qualities needed to fulfill his potential and secure the future of the kingdom.[12] With this in mind, Malhar Rao and Bajirao Peshwa approached Ahilya's father, Manakoji Shinde asking him for Ahilya's hand for his son Khande Rao. Manakoji Shinde was left speechless as he himself was looking for a suitable groom for her daughter. Ahilya's father never anticipated a proposal from such a high-ranking person. The only worry Ahilya's father had was how to match the level of that of a family like the Holkar's. But Malhar Rao asked Manakoji (Ahilya's father) to not worry about the expenses of marriage, rather mentioned how bright and meritorious Ahilya is. Their only ask was to give us their daughter as a future of their kingdom. Manakoji gladly accepted the offer with open arms. And that's how, in the year 1733,[13] Malhar Rao Holkar's son Khande Rao was married to Manakoji's daughter Ahilya amidst great fanfare.

The occasion was graced by Bajirao Peshwa himself. Malhar Rao was feeling fortunate to get such a virtuous daughter-in-law. And that's how a bright girl from a little hamlet Chondi became the daughter-in-law of Malwa. Ahilya's arrival at the Holkar palace gave birth to a new world steeped in grandeur and tradition where she was received with aarti by her four mothers-in-law— Gautamabai, Banabai, Dwarikabai, and Harkubai. Malhar Rao Holkar's first wife, Gautamabai, was the matriarch of the household, and was affectionately called *Baiji.* A woman who managed the vast Holkar estate with an unwavering sense of duty and with utmost discipline and grace. With passing days, Ahilyabai got familiarized with her new home, where she embraced her responsibilities

12 Jahagirdar Vijaya (2020), Karma Yogini: Life of Ahilyabai Holkar pg. 22 to 28.

13 Ibid

seamlessly and adapted to the family.[14] She was meticulous in even the smallest tasks by which Malhar Rao, was deeply impressed. Beyond completing her daily duties of the palace, Dubai, her sister-in-law became her quick confidante.[15]

Ahilyabai's journey had begun, not just as a member of the family but as a ruler who would leave a mark in the history of India. Ahilya's reign from 1765 to 1795 is remembered as a period of remarkable stability and prosperity. Even Jawaharlal Nehru praised her rule and described it as "almost legendary as a period during which perfect order and good government prevailed, and the people prospered."[16]

Her Daily Rituals and Life

Born into an ordinary family, Ahilya cherished many dreams about her future, from her education to her marriage. She never imagined that one day she would become the daughter-in-law of a kingdom. Adjusting to her new life and its roles brought many challenges to her, especially when it came to her husband. Initially, Khande Rao showed little inclination toward governance or military expeditions, preferring a life away from the responsibilities of the court. Yet, Ahilya, with her wisdom and patience, became a guiding force in his life. She encouraged him to engage with the affairs of the kingdom, fostering in him a sense of duty and purpose. Over time, Khande Rao began to take a more active role, although their relationship had its own course, Ahilya remained steadfast in her commitment to both him and the people.

---

14 Kadam, V.S(1993) , Maratha Confederacy, Munshiram Manoharlal Publishers ,New Delhi

15 Sardesai, G.S(1958), New History of the Marathas, Vol.II,III,Phoenix Publication ,Bombay

16 Nehru, J(1946), The Discovery of India (New York: John Day), 120.

The familial love she longed, staying away from her natal family was supplanted by the unwavering support of her mother-in-law, Gautamabai, and her father-in-law, who embraced her like their own daughter. To Ahilya, they became her real parents and guardians, offering her warmth and affection. Devi Ahilyabai Holkar was an early bird who started her day with morning prayers and performed the customary ceremonies which included the sacred sight of a black cow and Tulsi plant. She was an ardent listener of *Puranas*[17] and would emulate those practices in her daily life.[18] After breakfast which consisted of a vegetable diet, she again went to prayers and then took a short repose. Then dressing herself, always in a plain white sari, normally without a border, she went about two o'clock to her Darbar (Court) to attend to the state business till six in the evening.[19] By doing little things like telling the puranic moral tales to her husband, she showed him the righteous path.

Besides her serving attitude, she was endowed with fathomless love, pity, and a sense of renunciation. She had the art of making others a devotee by her behavior which helped Khande Rao to evolve. With the efforts of Ahilya, her

---

17 The term "Purana" means "ancient" in Sanskrit. These texts were composed over several centuries, with the earliest versions likely written between the 3rd and 10th centuries CE. There are 18 Maha Puranas (major Puranas) and 18 Up Puranas (minor Puranas). Each major Purana focuses on a central deity such as Vishnu or Shiva. Puranas typically cover five main subjects: the primary creation of the universe, secondary creation after periodic annihilation, genealogies of gods and patriarchs, the reigns of the Manus (the first humans), and the history of the solar and lunar dynasties. Puranas have played a crucial role in integrating local traditions into the broader Hindu framework, providing a synthesis of diverse beliefs and practices. Beyond mythology, Puranas impart moral and ethical lessons, emphasizing concepts like dharma (righteousness) and karma (action and its consequences). These texts have contributed significantly to Indian culture, serving as sources of knowledge on various subjects, including astronomy, medicine, and history.

18 Joshi, G.K(1978)., Ahilyabai Holkar (Jivan Charitra), 40-45.

19 ibid.

husband's interest grew in state affairs, and he even started accompanying his father to the battlefields. All this started off paying rich dividends where slowly and gradually he even perfected martial art. Thus, crossing all hurdles, Ahilyabai brought her married life to the right marital course. Soon after which, in 1745, they gave birth to their son, Maley Rao. The kingdom was all lightened up and dancing in the joy of the son. Malhar's joy was unmatched as he knew he had a prince for his kingdom now. Three years passed in the joy as Ahilya and Khande Rao's second child was born in 1748.[20] She was named Muktabai.

This was the period of Ahilya's golden days as she was in marital bliss and was endowed with two beautiful kids along with her in-laws by her side. With the unrelenting hard work, she transformed her husband and brought him to a course of righteousness. Hence, Ahilyabai brought good fortune to the family. Destiny could not fathom the fact that Ahilya was living her dream life. Golden rays of blessings in her married life were now covered by dark clouds of misfortune. Malhar Rao was impressed by his son's martial art skills and wanted to train him further to lead wars. In 1754, Khande Rao had accompanied Malhar Rao to recover taxes. They had recovered *Chauth* (land taxes) from almost all the principalities, but the king of Bharatpur, Suraj Mal Jat refused bluntly to pay the Chauth. The Rao's tried their best to deliberate upon this but to no avail. In response, they declared war.

The Battle of Kumbher

Kumbher, Deeg and Bharatpur together make the Yamuna Basin. It was the territory under the rule of Surajmal Jat. In

20 "Rajmata Ahilyabai Holkar." Indian Culture, n.d. Accessed on 23rd February 2025.

January 1754, Malhar Rao and Khande Rao Holkar declared war on Kumbher, laying siege to the fort.[21] Maratha soldiers were strategically positioned around the stronghold, with cannons primed for attack. Inside the fort, Surajmal's forces stood prepared, armed with artillery and ready for defense. As the battle commenced, Holkar's cannons and rifles roared, igniting an intense conflict that raged on for nearly six weeks without a decisive outcome. On March 17, 1754, a tragedy struck— the darkest day for the Holkar's.[22] A fierce battle between the Marathas and the Jats evoked a warfare emotion. Riding the horse in the battlefield, a bullet fired from the Jat army hit Khande Rao directly on his chest and he attained martyrdom. Malhar Rao, who was battling on the other side of the field was informed and this news shook him deeply. Tears spurted from his eyes. The Maratha force was deeply disturbed by this news. Bursting in tears at the news, the war came to a halt instantly.

Khande Rao was brought to a tent where the Rao family including Ahilya was present. Her sorrow had no limit. Her eyes kept on shedding tears. She began to wail beside the dead body. Malhar Rao gathered himself and forgot his own sorrow after seeing Ahilya's condition and consoled her. Grappled with sorrow and grief, Ahilyabai was convinced to commit Sati on her husband's pyre and expressed her desire to follow the traditional practice saying, "*He had pledged to accompany me lifelong; but he left me on the way. Hence, it is proper for me to commit Sati.*" [23] Malhar Rao came forward

21 Thakur V Vasudeo, Life and Life's work of Shree Devi Ahilya Bai Holkar , Holkar state History, printed by C.M, Shah Modern Printery Limited, Indore available on https://archive.org/details/in.ernet.dli.2015.199825/page/n5/mode/2up?view=theater accessed on September 26,2024.

22 ibid.

23 Dhariwal, L.C (1931),Indore State Gazatte, Indore

to convince Ahilya how important she is for the people of the state and the family. He requested Ahilya to be the pillar of strength in these difficult times. Lastly, he said, "*if you still don't change your mind, let me die first and let the kingdom suffer*," and added, "*You are Khande Rao for me and you have to control this kingdom and its wealth.*"[24] He mentioned how only Ahilya can help him forget the sorrow of his son's death. Malhar Rao broke into tears and fell at Ahilya's feet. hence, she was persuaded by Malhar Rao to give up her decision of committing *Sati*.[25] Despite all the sorrows, Ahilya took control of the daily affairs of the kingdom, and her efficiency and ability to work impressed her people. Her leadership skills and dedication earned her the respect and admiration of her subjects, ensuring that she remained a vital part of the kingdom's governance.[26]

As time progressed, Ahilyabai assumed comprehensive control over the finances, administration, correspondences, and recoveries, effectively managing all aspects of governance. During Malhar Rao's absences, she served as his representative overseeing daily operations on his behalf. The state responsibility and administration came on Ahilya's shoulders. Malhar Rao was fully aware of her capabilities to run administrative and political decisions. While on military expeditions, Malhar Rao corresponded with Ahilya through letters. The letters that Malhar Rao wrote to Ahilya revealed that she had gained enough expertise in politics and warfare. In Malhar Rao's absence, she managed the state to the best

24 Joshi, G.K., Ahilyabai Holkar (Jivan Charitra) (1978).

25 Zelliott Eleanor(2001), "Ahilyabai Holkar: A Magnificent Ruler, Saintly Administrator," Manushi, no. 124 p 10-11.

26 Soman Sangita and Jahagirdhar Vijaya, Karma Yogini(2021): Life of Ahilyabai Holkar, pp 30-35.

of her capabilities.[27] She sent fresh ration and military reinforcements for Malhar Rao in the battlefield and herself led several small military expeditions. Malhar Rao and Ahilya Bai exchanged several letters to keep each other posted about their whereabouts and conditions.[28]

Recognizing her exceptional administrative abilities, Malhar Rao Holkar took it upon himself to mentor his widowed daughter-in-law Ahilyabai, in both everyday governance and military leadership. In the few surviving letters, he wrote to her, the seasoned Maratha commander imparted invaluable wisdom drawn from his extensive battlefield experience. He advised her to always keep artillery within sight, to carefully assess the enemy's strength and numbers before deploying firepower, and to exercise patience and make her presence and reputation exert influence. He emphasized the principle of wielding minimal force while achieving maximum impact. Additionally, he urged her to move swiftly to Gwalior and personally oversee the production of guns and ammunition, ensuring the kingdom's military preparedness.

Ahilyabai was very principled in performing her duties as a ruler of the vast territory which included a large part of central India and territories to the north and south of Narmada,[29] a creation of her father-in-law Malhar Rao Holkar. We learn

27 Malcolm, J(1823), A Memoir of Central India: Including Malwa, and Adjoining Provinces, 50-55.

28 Ibid.

29 The Narmada River originates from the Amarkantak Plateau in Madhya Pradesh, at an elevation of approximately 1,057 meters (3,465 feet). It flows westward for about 1,312 kilometers (815 miles) through the states of Madhya Pradesh, Maharashtra, and Gujarat before emptying into the Arabian Sea via the Gulf of Khambhat near Bharuch.

from the accounts of Bharmal Dada[30] that she daily sat in open Darbar from two to six in the afternoon, when she was accessible to the commonest of her subjects. She attended the State business from nine to eleven in the night. She maintained this routine, save rare exceptions, till the end. When she took over the administration of Holkar's territory, its annual revenue was Rs.70 lacs. As a result of her wise policies and better management, the revenue of the state rose to Rs.1 crore 5 lacs.[31] Her thirty-year long reign witnessed peace and plenty, absence of famine, social harmony, a contented populace, and officials. It is creditable for Devi Ahilyabai that during her reign none of the Saranjami Sardars,[32] who held 36 *mahals*, questioned her authority, and they remained loyal and respectful towards her. Devi Ahilyabai was very solicitous about the rights and welfare of her subjects of whichever rank

30 Bharmal Dada was a trusted personal attendant and confidant of Devi Ahilyabai Holkar, the revered queen of the Malwa kingdom. He served her for over thirty years and provided valuable insights into her daily life and governance. His accounts highlight Ahilyabai's commitment to her duties, her spiritual practices, and her role as a leader. Bharmal Dada described how Ahilyabai would rise before dawn to perform her morning prayers and rituals, including paying homage to a black cow and a Tulsi plant. He viewed her as an incarnation of a deity, emphasizing her piety and dedication to her responsibilities. His observations were later shared by Sir John Malcolm, an eminent historian and civil servant, who helped document Ahilyabai's legacy and contributions to Indian history. Through Bharmal Dada's accounts, we gain a deeper understanding of Ahilyabai's character, her administrative acumen, and her devotion to the welfare of her people, solidifying her status as one of India's most respected historical figures.

31 Zelliott E (2001), "Ahilyabai Holkar: A Magnificent Ruler, Saintly Administrator," Manushi, no. 124 : 10-11.

32 Saranjami Sardars were feudal lords or military chiefs in the Maratha Empire, entrusted with the administration and military responsibilities of specific territories known as mahals. These Sardars held their lands under the Saranjam system, a form of land grant provided by the state in exchange for military service and loyalty. The Saranjam system was introduced by Malhar Rao Holkar and was recognized for its efficiency in managing resources and maintaining order within the Maratha Confederacy. During Ahilyabai Holkar's reign (1767–1795), 36 mahals were managed by Saranjami Sardars under her governance. Despite holding significant autonomy, these Sardars remained loyal to Ahilyabai and did not rebel against her authority— a testament to her diplomatic and administrative skills. She ensured that the Saranjam system functioned smoothly, balancing power between the central administration and regional chiefs, while maintaining peace and stability in her kingdom.

they might be. As Sir John Malcolm writes, "*She heard every complaint in person, and was always accessible, patient and unwearied in the investigation of most insignificant cases when appeals were made for her decision. ... She gave a large part of central India peace and good administration during a most turbulent period and her 30 yearlong rule is regarded as a model of benevolent and effective government.*" [33]

Devi Ahilya's Succession

Malhar Rao Holkar was deeply affected by the death of Khanderao Holkar in the battle of Kumbher. His health deteriorated as he could not bear the loss of his only son. After a period of mourning and illness, Malhar Rao breathed his last in Alampur at the age of 73[34]. For Ahilya, her father-in-law was more than just a guardian by marriage— he was an affectionate father, a guiding guru, and a revered ruler who shaped her understanding of governance and duty. However, with his passing, Ahilyabai not only lost a pillar of emotional support but also her stronghold in political leadership. This loss was a severe blow, shaking the very foundation of her life. Everything around her seemed to bc unraveling, and the world she had so carefully nurtured felt as fragile as shattered glass. In this moment of turmoil, her only source of hope and strength was her beloved son, Malerao. Yet, fate had yet another cruel trial in store for her, as destiny seemed determined to test her resilience once again.

33 Thakur V Vasudeo, Life and Life's work of Shree Devi Ahilya Bai Holkar , Holkar state History, printed by C.M, Shah Modern Printery Limited, Indore available on https://archive.org/details/in.ernet.dli.2015.199825/page/n5/mode/2up?view=theater accessed on September 26,2024.

34 Thakur V Vasudeo, Life and Life's work of Shree Devi Ahilya Bai Holkar , Holkar state History, printed by C.M, Shah Modern Printery Limited, Indore available on https://archive.org/details/in.ernet.dli.2015.199825/page/n5/mode/2up?view=theater accessed on September 26,2024.

Maley Rao, like many born into prosperity, initially exhibited traits of impulsiveness and restlessness. However, under Ahilyabai's unwavering guidance, he was nurtured with discipline and a strong sense of responsibility. Recognizing the importance of shaping him into a capable leader, she imparted lessons in governance, military strategy, and statecraft, instilling in him the values of justice and duty. Following Malhar Rao's passing, Maley Rao was crowned as the Subedar on August 23, 1766.[35] Though young and still gaining experience, Ahilyabai stood by his side, ensuring the kingdom's stability while patiently mentoring him. She believed in his potential and remained committed to refining his abilities, guiding him to uphold the legacy of the Holkar dynasty with wisdom and strength. Ahilya always expected his son to walk on the righteous path like her father-in-law and like how she transformed her husband. Ahilya constantly worried about the fame and legacy of her lineage, even in her letters written to her son she emphasized on how he should run the kingdom prudently like his grandfather did.

Fate had a different plan for Maley Rao, he became a victim of manipulation and deceit and killed an innocent person thinking that the person was a threat to his kingdom. Upon learning of the innocence of the murdered person, he was consumed by guilt and remorse, leading to a decline in his mental and physical health.[36] Every possible effort was made to heal him. From sacred prayers and Vedic rituals to offerings at temples and consultations with esteemed healers, Ahilyabai spared no means in seeking his recovery. For nine long months, she held onto hope, tirelessly performing every

35 Ibid

36 Kumar, N (2023), Lokmata Ahilyabai Holkar, Adhyayan Books, 40-45.

rite believed to restore health and prolong life. Yet, despite her unwavering devotion and relentless efforts, fate had its own course. Malerao succumbed to his illness at the tender age of twenty-two, leaving behind a grieving mother and a kingdom in sorrow. In an ultimate act of devotion, his two wives chose to commit Sati on his funeral pyre, embracing the flames as a testament to their loyalty and sacrifice. Since Maley Rao had no son, the debate on his successor arose. People of Holkar kingdom had already started addressing Ahilya as "Devi Ahilya." They wished to see her take over the kingdom. They believed in her and saw how she has been running the kingdom over the past years. During Malhar Rao's time, Ahilya was the one looking after the kingdom as Malhar Rao was always at the battlefield. After his death, she took care of all administrative tasks as her son was young and untrained. Therefore, it was nothing but natural for the people of the kingdom to want Ahilya to be the ruler. However, few men in the kingdom could not fathom the fact that a woman that too, "a widow woman" would take over the throne. The *Diwan* of the kingdom Gangadhar Yashwant Chandrachur[37] who earlier supported Ahilya, was against her becoming the ruler. For such men, this also was against the scriptures and their teachings.[38] Devi Ahilya was taken aback by Gangadhar's opinion as he was one of the most trusted allies. Gangadhar

37 Gangadhar Yashwant Chandrachud, commonly known as Gangoba Tatya, served as the Diwan of Malhar Rao Holkar, a prominent leader in the Maratha Empire. His rise to power began from relatively humble origins as a small-time Patil near Khed in Pune. Over time, he gained prominence and became a key figure in the administration of the Holkar dynasty. As Diwan, Gangoba played a significant role in the political landscape of the Maratha Empire, particularly during a tumultuous period marked by internal conflicts and external threats. He was involved in military campaigns and was known for his strategic influence within the Holkar administration.

38 Nagrale, N. N (1979). Ahilyabai and her benevolent administration, Proceedings of the Indian History Congress Vol.40.pp 700-706. Indian History Congress retrived on www.jstor.org/stable/44142013

advised Ahilya to adopt a son and make him the new subedar of the kingdom. She understood the diplomacy and betrayal in his suggestion. The enthronement of a minor (adopted son– as Gangadhar wanted) as a subedar would require Ahilya to surrender from all her administrative roles and thus all the powers would be transferred to Gangadhar.

She stood against the suggestion given by Gangadhar and said, "*I am the daughter-in-law, wife and a mother of the people who have ruled the kingdom. It is, therefore, not only my inherent right, but a duty that I must take the administration of the kingdom in my hands in such a difficult situation and discharge my responsibility of removing the miseries of the people of my state.*"[39] Gangadhar and the colleagues (men of the state) were infuriated by this statement and they took this to their ego and said, "*how can a widow rule our kingdom in our presence. It is daring for a frail woman to challenge us like this.*"[40] In retaliation, Gangadhar informed Raghunath Rao[41] through a letter that after the death of Maley Rao, the kingdom had no legitimate successor. He said, "come with a strong force and capture the kingdom." (Burway, M. W (1925)) Raghunath Rao, also known as Raghoba Dada was a man hungry for power, therefore for him this was a great opportunity to acquire a kingdom, and he immediately directed his force towards Indore. While backstabbing Ahilya, Gangadhar underestimated her strength. Ahilya's soldiers were informing her about the vicious moves Gangadhar was planning against her. She was also aware that Raghoba Dada

39 Kumar, N (2023), Lokmata Ahilyabai Holkar Adhyayan Books, 40-45.

40 Kibe M. V (1939)., "The Cultural Indian Empire of the Saintly Queen Ahilyabai Holkar," Proceedings of the Indian History Congress 3: 1330–1333.

41 Raghunath Rao, also known as Raghobadada, was a prominent figure in the Maratha Empire and the uncle of Peshwa Madhav Rao.

and his fifty thousand people army was coming towards Indore. Yet Ahilya remained clear on her resolution. She said, "*when a frail woman takes a firm resolution, she can humiliate even the strongest of men.*"[42] She at once resolved to destroy the vicious plans by both Gangadhar and Raghobadada. She announced, *"No one should take me for granted, that I am a woman, a frail woman or a widow woman and that they can't suppress me easily. I am invincible to anybody if I stand in the battlefield. We are the subedar of Peshwa and are always ready to defeat and serve our kingdom. And that it would not be possible for anybody to usurp the Holkar kingdom in all three ages. My father-in-law did not acquire it, he won the kingdom. He won it with his strength and sword. We will not spare the life of anybody who dares to eye our kingdom menacingly.*" [43] Summoning her trusted men, Ahilya declared to take over the kingdom and its administration. This caused a wave of enthusiasm and power amongst the people of the kingdom, except a few. People had blind faith in her. Devi Ahilya then intimated her commander-in-chief Tukoji Rao of the whole facade and instructed him to ensure the safety of the people of the kingdom. She then sent out letters to Mahadji Scindia, Bhosale, Gaekwad, and other commanders to inform them about the emergency and remind them about the services and assistance required. In reply, all commanders expressed their anger and came in support of Ahilya and the kingdom with their fullest cooperation.[44] Ahilya was also keen on having an army of women, so she wrote a letter to Shrimant Madhav Rao Peshwa and intimated him about the conspiracy

42 Malcolm, J (1823), A Memoir of Central India: Including Malwa, and Adjoining Provinces, 50-55.

43 Burway, Muntazim Bahadur M. W (1925)., Life of His Highness Maharaja Tukoji Rao Holkar II, GCSI, Ruler of Indore (1835-1886). Accession Number: E17723

44 Ibid.

of Gangadhara. Madhav Rao, a very just and righteous ruler in himself told Ahilya, "*Should someone launch an attack on the kingdom against him and drive him away.*" (please check this quote) Along with his support, Ahilya formed an army of five hundred women. She then started training the women army and taught them how to use the weapons that can help in the war.

As the preparations were going on, news arrived that Raghoba Dada had arrived in Ujjain and was camping with fifty thousand people whilst waiting for more force, that he had invited, through letters for help. Not only nobody showed up as they all refused to fight against Ahilya, but the reinforcements arrived to support Ahilya.[45] With this began a war of diplomatic heft and strategy. Tukoji Rao had warned Raghobadada to not enter their territory. Ahilya also wrote a letter to Raghobadada where she had written, "*You have come here with an evil intention of taking over my kingdom. You think I am a weak woman, but your intentions will never materialize. But you will come to know about my strength and forces. Nobody will blame me if I lose but nobody will praise you for your victory either. And if you lose you will never be able to show your face anywhere. Because as a man the blemish of attacking a weak woman can never be wiped out. Remember this while you are entering the battlefield.*" [46]

The letter by Ahilya and the war preparations by her made him doubt his next steps. He decided against fighting her. He then sent a letter to the commander-in-chief, Tukoji Rao where he

---

45 Nagrale, N. N (1979). Ahilyabai and her benevolent administration, Proceedings of the Indian History Congress Vol.40.pp 700-706. Indian History Congress retrived on www.jstor.org/stable/44142013

46 Burway, M. B. M. W. (1925). Life of His Highness Maharaja Tukoji Rao Holkar II, GCSI, Ruler of Indore (1835-1886). Holkar State Printing Press.

said, "*you have mistaken us that we are here to fight or attack the Holkar kingdom. Our past relations with Malhar Rao have been very loyal and we can never fight against their daughter-in-law. We have in fact come here to give condolences to Ahilya after the death of his son.*"[47] Raghobadada with his wife and some commanders left to visit the Holkar kingdom where he first met Tukoji Rao who greeted them respectfully. Ahilya too gave them a warm traditional welcome. They both had lengthy conversations. Raghobadada stayed for a month and during that month he came to know more about Ahilya. Impressed by her personality, he never discussed the issue of adopting a successor again. Devi Ahilya took a firm hold on the administration of the kingdom.

47 Kibe M. V(1939):., "The Cultural Indian Empire of the Saintly Queen Ahilyabai Holkar," Proceedings of the Indian History Congress 3 1330–1333.

CHAPTER - 2

Ahilyabai Holkar: An epitome of Inclusive Justice

Ahilyabai Holkar was not just a visionary ruler but an epitome of justice, who ensured fairness for all, regardless of status or rank. Her commitment and belief in righteousness can be justified with striking incidents of the past that remain etched in history. The archival account titled "Karanataka Devi Shree Ahilyabai Holkar"[48] presents a compelling story that underscores Ahilyabai Holkar's unwavering commitment to justice. It recounts an incident when an injured calf suddenly leaped onto the path that Maloji Rao was passing. Oblivious to its suffering, Maloji continued his journey. Later, Ahilyabai passed through the same path and noticed a grieving cow sitting beside its lifeless calf. The sight troubled her so much that she inquired about the incident and was appalled to learn of her son's indifference. Without hesitation, she summoned her daughter-in-law, Meenabai, to court and posed a question: "If someone kills a son in front of his mother, what punishment should he receive?" Without realizing the weight of her response, Meenabai firmly declared, "Such a

48 Thakur V Vasudeo, Life and Life's work of Shree Devi Ahilya Bai Holkar , Holkar state History, printed by C.M, Shah Modern Printery Limited, Indore available on https://archive.org/details/in.ernet.dli.2015.199825/page/n5/mode/2up?view=theater accessed on September 26,2024.

person deserves the death penalty."[49] Ahilyabai commanded the same punishment for her own son which showed how strongly she believed in the principles of justice. However, when the time came to carry out the sentence, none of the charioteers had the heart to drive the chariot that would seal Maloji's fate. Determined to uphold the law, Ahilyabai took the reins herself. As she drove the chariot forward, the grieving mother—the cow stepped in front, blocking the path. The site where this profound event took place, near Rajbada, came to be known as "Aada Bazaar"— a testament to a ruler who upheld justice with unwavering fairness, yet understood the power of compassion. This incident proves, she was an embodiment of divine qualities and with a profound sense of fairness and righteousness, proving that no one, not even her own son, was above the law.

Muktabai's Marriage and Its Significance

Devi Ahilya's daughter Muktabai was the only person to remain with her after the deaths of her mother, father-in-law, husband, and son. She loved her dearly. Devi Ahilya was looking for a suitable groom for her now that she was an adult. Due to family issues and political unpredictability, Devi Ahilya has not been able to make a genuine attempt to arrange Muktabai's marriage so far. Devi Ahilya prioritized administrative reforms after seizing power of the kingdom and moved the capital to Maheshwar. Political unpredictability, a decline in law and order, and the widespread fear of robbers and thieves had left the state's administration in complete

49 Nagrale, N. N (1979). Ahilyabai and her benevolent administration, Proceedings of the Indian History Congress Vol.40.pp 700-706. Indian History Congress retrived on www.jstor.org/stable/44142013

disorder. People were living in fear of robbers and thieves. In order to reassure her citizens and bolster law and order, Devi Ahilya called all the important chieftains, officials, soldiers, and people to her court, where they engaged in a heated debate over the matter. She said in court that she was calling on them to eradicate the state's robbers. She said, "*Whoever exterminates the robbers in the state and relieves my subjects from their fear, I will marry my only daughter to him.*"[50] Caste and creed, high and low status, poverty, and wealth, had a significant impact on marriage arrangements back then. Devi Ahilya, however, had vowed to wed her only daughter to a man of such courage who would put an end to the kingdom's banditry. Therefore, while choosing a husband for her only daughter, she placed greater value on bravery than on birth or tribe. She put her only daughter on the line and set the highest example of renunciation and dedication for the good of her subjects because she believed that bravery was the greatest merit, surpassing all other distinctions such as caste and creed, high and low rank, poverty, and wealth. The whole court stood in silence after hearing the declaration of Devi Ahilya. For a while, nobody came forward to accept the challenge.

Yashwant Rao Fanase, a young man, abruptly stood up. He bravely accepted the task, but he made it clear that he would need resources and personnels to complete the job. Devi Ahilya silently praised the young man and gave him all the money and forces he needed. Yashwant Fanase was a brave and intellectual man. Acting bravely, he quickly put an end

50 Thakur V Vasudeo, Life and Life's work of Shree Devi Ahilya Bai Holkar , Holkar state History, printed by C.M, Shah Modern Printery Limited, Indore available on https://archive.org/details/in.ernet.dli.2015.199825/page/n5/mode/2up?view=theater accessed on September 26,2024.

to the fear of bandits and thieves and restored peace to the realm. He had demonstrated that he was the most suitable husband for Devi Ahilya's daughter. Devi Ahilya kept her word and married her daughter Muktabai to Yashwant Rao Fanase. Everyone in Maheshwar was invited to the ceremony.

Military Expeditions during her reign

Ahilya Bai's war strategies has always helped the kingdom from the time of Malhar Rao. During her correspondence with Ahilya, Malhar Rao taught her the intricacies of war time strategies and took into consideration her inputs during his expeditions. On one such occasion during Malhar Rao's time, the Rampura Pargana[51] in Rajasthan which shared a boundary with the Holkar Kingdom was brewing with internal fight for power. Chandravat Rajput[52] who were descended from the Rana clans of Udaipur, lived in the area. Their participation in the Holkar Kingdom was not a recent

51 Rampura Pargana is a historical region in the Malwa territory of Madhya Pradesh, India, which holds significance in the context of the Holkar dynasty, particularly during the reign of Ahilya Bai Holkar. As a part of her administration, Rampura Pargana was one of the many parganas (administrative divisions) that she governed. During her rule from 1767 to 1795, Ahilya Bai was known for her effective governance and efforts to promote economic development, social welfare, and cultural advancements. She established a network of administrative units like Rampura Pargana to ensure efficient management of her kingdom. This area would have been integral to her strategies for maintaining control and fostering prosperity in her realm.

52 The Chandravat Rajput are a historical clan that is part of the broader Rajput community in India. They are associated with the Sisodia dynasty and have a significant presence in the Rampura region of Neemuch district in Madhya Pradesh. The Chandravat Rajput trace their lineage back to the Sisodia rulers of Udaipur, which adds to their historical prestige. The history of Chandravat Rajputs is marked by their conflicts with the Holkar dynasty, particularly during the reign of Ahilya Bai Holkar. Tensions arose when Malhar Rao Holkar was granted control over Rampura, in exchange for aiding Maharaja Madhav Singh of Jaipur, a decision that was not accepted by the Chandravat Rajputs, who considered Rampura their rightful territory. This disagreement led to multiple uprisings by the Chandravats against Holkar rule, which were successfully suppressed by Ahilya Bai.

development. Madhav Singh and Ishwari Singh are the two sons of Sawai Jai Singh, the king of Jaipur. A power battle broke out between them after Jai Singh's demise. At that time, Madhav Singh was residing in Udaipur with his maternal uncle Rana Sangram Singh, who was Chandravanshi. Sangram Singh had given Madhav Singh some territorial areas for sustenance. In the absence of Madhav Singh, Ishwari Singh occupied the throne in Jaipur. This led to a power struggle between the two brothers. But he lacked the power to defeat Ishwari Singh. Hence, they had sought the help of Malhar Rao to obtain their ruling right. Accepting the just right of Madhav Singh, Malhar Rao ensured him of all possible assistance and wrote to Ishwari Singh instructing him to surrender the throne to his brother Madhav Singh or face a war. Fearing Malhar Rao, Ishwari Singh committed suicide, and Madhav Singh got his rights. As a thanksgiving, Madhav Singh presented Malhar Rao with sixty-four lakh rupees plus the area of Rampura that his uncle had given him. Madhav Singhs' cousin (son of Rana Sangram Singh) objected to the fact that he had given the Holkar a portion of Chandravat's realm without their consent. However, they were unable to challenge Malhar Rao's authority at the time. However, Chandravats of Rampura would periodically rise in rebellion to gain freedom from Holkar's control after Malhar Rao's death. Devi Ahilya, however, would always put a halt to their uprising by sending an army there right away. The Chandravats' uprising was never successful because they lacked the backing of other Rajput lords in Rajasthan. The Holkar Kingdom" army terrified the Rajput monarchs of Rajasthan, as the state was also home to Mahadji Scindia's large army. Because of the combined strength of Holkar and Scindia, Rajput kings hesitated to openly support the revolt of

Chandravats. But the fire of discontent had been smoldering in the hearts of Rajputs against Marathas. They had been waiting for the right opportunity, when suddenly they got a golden chance by sheer luck. In the battle of Lalsot,[53] Mahadji Scindia lost. As a result, his army left Rajasthan, and the Marathas' grip on Rajputana weakened. Rajput powers seized the chance and started banding together to fight the Marathas. The simmering embers of dissatisfaction quickly transformed into fiery flares that were prepared to destroy the Maratha power. All of these developments gave the Chandravats in Rampura more boldness as well. To escape Holkar's control, they also started flailing their limbs.[54] Consequently, thick, powerful clouds of conflict started to build up at the Holkar Kingdom's edge. To overthrow and expel Maratha hegemony, Rajput swords started to brandish.

This time, when Chandravats rose in revolt, Devi Ahilya's commander-in-chief Subedar Tukoji Rao was away in the far south leading a war expedition. Chandravats had anticipated that in the absence of Tukoji Rao, Devi Ahilya would not be able to face them, and they would get an easy victory. But

53 The Battle of Lalsot was fought in May 1787 between the Rajputs of Jaipur and Jodhpur against the Marathas, led by Mahadji Scindia. The conflict arose from Mahad Ji's demand for a substantial tax of Rs. 63,00,000 from the Jaipur court, which they refused to pay. In response, Mahadji marched against Jaipur with his forces. The battle began with artillery exchanges, as both sides utilized their cannons. The Jaipur army, equipped with long-range artillery, adopted a defensive stance. However, the Rathore horsemen from Jodhpur grew impatient and launched a charge against the Maratha forces, causing significant casualties on both sides. Despite their bravery, the Rathore's faced challenges as they were pushed back due to reinforcements arriving for the Marathas. The battle did not yield a decisive victory for either side. Mahadji Scindia retreated due to internal dissensions within his ranks and supply failures. The Rajputs also suffered heavy losses, particularly among the Jodhpur forces, which lost over a thousand horsemen. Ultimately, while the battle was marked by intense fighting and high casualties, it did not result in a clear outcome, and subsequently both armies returned to their camps after failing to achieve their objectives.

54 Burway, M. B. M. W. (1925). *Life of His Highness Maharaja Tukoji Rao Holkar II, GCSI, Ruler of Indore (1835-1886)*. Holkar State Printing Press.

they were wrong. Little were they aware of skills and military strength of Devi Ahilya, who had full knowledge of their movements, had prepared an action plan to deal with them. She instructed all the chieftains to keep the forces prepared. She prepared her army and arranged ration, ammunition and explosives for the battlefront. Associate Maratha chieftains and Shrimant Peshwa[55] in Poona too were intimated about the development. While Devi Ahilya was busy in war preparations, Shivaji Nana, in charge of Nimba Hera fortress[56] which was situated in Rampura Pargana arrived. He had fled deserting the fortress. Shivaji Nana told Ahilyabai that there were only one hundred Maratha soldiers in the fortress and two thousand Rajput soldiers had attacked the fortress, "*Hence I deserted the fortress*."[57] Shivaji Nana also informed that the forces of Udaipur's Rana had invaded the Holkar Kingdom up to Chakharda, and Jagirdar Chandravat of Rampura had joined the rebels against the domination of Holkar. Devi Ahilya was infuriated at Shivaji Nana and roaring with anger she said, *"Shivaji Nana, fleeing from the*

55 The title Shrimant Peshwa refers to the prime ministers of the Maratha Empire, who eventually became the de facto rulers of the confederacy. The Peshwas were instrumental in shaping the empire's administration, military strategies, and territorial expansion. The term "Shrimant" was an honorific used to denote their high status

56 The Nimbahera Fortress is a historical fort located in the Chittorgarh district of Rajasthan, India. It holds significant importance due to its strategic location and historical context, particularly during the 18th century when it was involved in the power struggles between various regional powers, including the Marathas and Rajputs. Originally built as a stronghold, Nimbahera Fortress served as a military base and played a crucial role in the defense against invasions. The fort's architecture reflects the typical style of Rajputana forts, characterized by robust walls and strategic positioning on elevated terrain, which provided a vantage point for surveillance and defense. During the time of Ahilya Bai Holkar, the fortress was significant in the broader context of Maratha expansion and control in Rajasthan. The Marathas sought to consolidate their power in the region, and forts like Nimbahera were vital for maintaining military presence and influence over local territories.

57 Nagrale, N. N (1979). Ahilyabai and her benevolent administration, Proceedings of the India☺n History Congress Vol.40.pp 700-706. Indian History Congress retrived on www.jstor.org/stable/44142013

fortress instead of countering the enemies, you have shown great cowardice. You would have attained heaven, had you died confronting the enemies instead of fleeing. And if you had any fear that Ahilyabai would get you decapitated, you would not have dared to run away. Your behavior has only added to the courage of the enemy. Now they are attacking us with double enthusiasm. It is all an outcome of your blunder." Just then a messenger brought the news that with ten thousand soldiers, Rana had launched massive attacks on the villages in Nimbahera, Javad and the adjoining areas, and Ambaji Pant, whom Devi Ahilya had sent to counter the enemies, were killed in a battle near Chakharda. Hearing the news, Devi said, "*Look Nana, how your cowardice has increased the enthusiasm of Chandravats. Had you countered them from the beginning they would not have dared to come so far.*"[58]

Devi said, "*It is not the first revolt of Chandravati. After the death of the late Subedar Malhar Rao, when Tukoji Rao was in the South, they had risen in revolt in 1771 taking full advantage of the occasion. We had a fierce battle near the village Palsuda on the north of Mandsaur. With a sword in hand, I had myself taken part in the battle. After much bloodshed, Chandravats were defeated. Defeat of the enemy depends upon how much we are prepared for a bloodshed only to win the war. In 1783 also, when they had revolted, we made every arrangement to deal with them. Rajputs are taking my magnanimity as my weakness, hence this time I will have to decide over their fate forever.*"[59]

58 Nagrale, N. N (1979). Ahilyabai and her benevolent administration, Proceedings of the Indian History Congress Vol.40.pp 700-706. Indian History Congress retrived on www.jstor.org/stable/44142013

59 Burway, M. B. M. W. (1925). Life of His Highness Maharaja Tukoji Rao Holkar II, GCSI, Ruler of Indore (1835-1886). Holkar State Printing Press.

Devi Ahilya made the decision to dispatch a sizable army to control Chandravats' periodic uprisings. Her army launched a massive attack on Rajputs. Devi herself reached the battlefield and began to direct the soldiers from behind. She also carried out fresh recruitments to reinforce the dead and injured forces. She also supervised the treatment of the injured' and rewarded the soldiers who showed extraordinary courage. Thus, skilled leadership of Devi Ahilya and encouragement led to a generation of exceptional enthusiasm in the Holkar army. Forces launched a massive attack on the Rajput army. A fierce battle followed. Thousands of people died on both sides. Forces of Devi Ahilya uprooted the feet of the Rajput army. In no time, Rajput forces began to run for their lives, victorious forces of Holkar reached Rampura and recaptured it. Leader of the rebel Chandravats fled and took refuge in the fort of Amad. Devi's forces surrounded the fort. Devi's forces had a very famous gun '*Iwala*'[60] Cannons fired by Iwala were showering destruction on the fort. At last, Devi's forces vanquished the fort and captured Saubhag Singh Chandrawal, the leader of the rebels. By the order of Devi Ahilya, he was tied to the barrel of the gun and blown up. All the rebels surrendered and put down their arms, thus, with firm determination Devi Ahilya crushed the rebellion. When the news of Devi Ahilya's victory reached Poona, Shrimant Peshwa celebrated a victory festival. Guns were fired in the honor of Devi. Famous political, diplomat and savant courtier of Peshwa, Nana Fadnavis said, "*So far, we have heard about the praises of Devi Ahilya's compassion. But we did not know that she is an amazon, who can rout her*

60 The famous gun known as Iwala was a significant piece of artillery used by Devi Ahilya Bai Holkar during her reign as the queen of Indore. This gun exemplified the advanced artillery capabilities of the Maratha Empire at the time and was a symbol of Ahilya Bai's military strength and strategic prowess.

enemies. But today, we came to know that Maheshwar is a gateway of Poona on the bank of Narmada."[61]

Nana Fadnavis[62] was the 'think tank' of Shrimant Peshwa. He had the greatest influence on contemporary history. Such a great personality was an admirer of Devi Ahilya and respected her. Chandravats had risen three times in revolt. First time in 1771, second time in 1783, and third time in 1787. On all the three occasions Devi Ahilya herself crushed the revolt. In 1771 she herself took part in the battle. In 1783 she sent an army to deal with the rebels, while in 1787, despite her old age she led her forces directly in the battlefield and steely crushed the revolt forever.[63] On all the three occasions, her commander-in-chief was away in the far South. Hence, Devi Ahilya had to fight these battles on her own strength. But working with super strategic understanding and cleverness she defeated seemingly indomitable enemies. All these victories led to an ever-increasing popularity of her ability, diplomacy, and gallantry throughout the country.

The Passing of Heirs: A Kingdom in Mourning (Muktabai and her son Nathyaba)

In 1767, Muktabai, the daughter of Devi Ahilyabai, had given

---

61 Nagrale, N. N (1979). Ahilyabai and her benevolent administration, Proceedings of the Indian History Congress Vol.40.pp 700-706. Indian History Congress retrieved on www.jstor.org/stable/44142013.

62 Nana Fadnavis, born Balaji Janardan Bhanu in 1742, was a prominent statesman and minister of the Maratha Empire. He played a crucial role in the political landscape of the Maratha Confederacy during a tumultuous period following the Third Battle of Panipat in 1761. His exceptional intelligence and political acumen earned him the nickname "Maratha Machiavelli" due to his strategic prowess in governance and diplomacy.

63 Burway, M. B. M. W. (1925). Life of His Highness Maharaja Tukoji Rao Holkar II, GCSI, Ruler of Indore (18☺35-1886). Holkar State Printing Press.

birth to a son. His name was Nathyaba.[64] Devi Ahilya was overjoyed when her grandson was born. Devi had no rightful heir to her kingdom because her son Maley Rao had passed away without leaving any children. It was only natural for her to feel pleased when her daughter gave birth to a son under such circumstances. Her fondness for her grandchildren is therefore greater than that for her own children. Furthermore, Nathyaba gained Devi Ahilya's affection because he was the sole son. Devi kept him close to her most of the time. She fostered him with great love and care and tried to culture him with good customs. She had a desire to make him the successor of the kingdom. Since infancy, Nathyaba has been extremely frail and prone to illness. Devi tried everything to get him healthier, but he did not respond, thus there was no way to get him healthier. Nathyaba contracted tuberculosis when he was twenty-one years old. He had a cough and a fever for two years straight. The only thing left of his body was the skeleton. He was treated in vain by numerous Vaidya and Hakeems. He was unable to get better. Tuberculosis was considered an incurable disease back then. No Vaidya or Hakeem had an effective treatment for this deadly disease. Even Shrimant Madhav Rao Peshwa had died because of tuberculosis.[65] Only the name of tuberculosis was enough to unnerve a person. Devi Ahilya made every effort to get Nathyaba cured, but to no avail. The illness kept spreading. Devi turned to charity after charmers, Vaidya, Hakeems, and other treatments failed in the hopes that Nathyaba may be cured with the help of the impoverished, saints, sages, Brahmins, and others. Devi focused all her hopes on her

64 Ibid.

65 Nagrale, N. N (1979). Ahilyaবai and her benevolent administration, Proceedings of the Indian History Congress Vol.40.pp 700-706. Indian History Congress retrieved on www.jstor.org/stable/44142013

sole grandchild, Nathyaba, following the death of her son. She did everything she could to heal Nathyaba in the hopes that he would one day be held accountable for the kingdom. Ahilya started observing fasts; recited the Lord's name and even pledged to make suitable offerings to please the God. Devi Ahilya did everything for the health of her grandson. She even donated gold equal to the weight of Nathyaba.[66] But all her efforts proved futile. Nathyaba's health was getting worse every day. Devi received support from the people of Maheshwar as well. In the temples, Kirtans and recitations went on. Even the chants of *Mahamrityunjaya* were recited. However, nothing was effective. At the young age of twenty-three, Devi Ahilya's grandson Nathyaba passed away on November 15, 1790.[67] His two wives, ages ten and seventeen, respectively, his parents, Muktabai and Yashwant Rao Fanase, and his elderly grandmother, Devi Ahilya, survived him.

Untimely death of their only son proved a severe blow for the son-in-law and daughter of Devi Ahilyabai. Their condition became critical. Yashwant Rao Fanase's mental state worsened to the point where he lost all sense of enjoyment in life. He was overcome by anguish day and night. In the end, grieving caused his health to deteriorate as well. His condition did not improve with any treatment. A year after Nathyaba's passing, on November 3, 1791, Yashwant Rao Fanase also passed away unexpectedly from cholera.[68] Devi has lost her only daughter to widowhood. Deep sadness engulfed the entire Maheshwar. Devi Ahilya's grief knew no bounds.

66 Keay, J, India: A History (New York: Grove Press, 2000).

67 Nath, R(1995), Indore: The City of Ahilyabai Holkar Jaipur: Historical Research Documentation Programme.

68 Belly, Jhona(1975), Ahilyabai A poem, Shri Kshatriya Dhangar Sewa Sanstha,Indore

She started crying uncontrollably. Even the final pillar of her life had collapsed at sixty-six. Devi's daughter abruptly informed her of her choice to commit Sati with him.[69] This decision completely broke Devi Ahilya. With only Muktabai as her last support, her committing Sati, meant the end of Devi Ahilya's whole lineage. After her mother and father, in-laws, husband, son, brother, daughters-in-law, grandson, granddaughters-in-law, now her son-in-law and daughter too were leaving her. Devi Ahilya tried hard to convince her daughter that considering her old age, she must give up her decision to commit Sati. But all her insistence failed. Muktabai stayed firm to her resolution. She said, "*Mother, we two are the only survivors of our family. You will have no support after me, and I will have no support after you. At the time of our father's death, you had resolved to commit Sati. But at our grandfather's request and to look after the kingdom after him, you had changed your mind. You had a purpose to live your life. But I have no purpose in life. As far as your looking after is concerned, there are many people to look after you. Besides, much of life has passed. But if I don't commit Sati today, it would be extremely difficult for me to live a purposeless life. Hence, it is better for me to commit Sati on the pyre of my husband.*"[70]

Devi Ahilya had no reply to the logic of Muktabai, who was firm in her resolution. On one hand, the hearse of Yashwant Rao was being decorated and on the other Muktabai was being adorned as a Sati. Scenes of Yashwant Rao's funeral procession were very tragic. His relatives, officials and thousands of citizens were walking mournfully

69 Sen, S.N(1 January 2017) An Advanced History of Modern India Primus Books

70 Burway, M. B. M. W. (1925). Life of His Highness Maharaja Tukoji Rao Holkar II, GCSI, Ruler of Indore (1835-1886). Holkar State Printing Press.

in the procession. Muktabai's face was glowing with an extraordinary sheen. With folded hands, she was walking slowly behind the bier. Behind her and supported by many maidservants, was Devi Ahilya walking slowly. On the rear side of the procession, was a huge crowd shouting Jai Sati Mata. For Yashwant Rao Fanase, a massive sandalwood pyre was built on the Narmada banks. They put his body on the pyre. Muktabai also took her husband's head on her lap while sitting on the pyre. Divine radiance shone in Muktabai's face.[71] The pyre was set on fire amid the loud sounds of musical instruments and the recital of Vedic hymns. The sounds of drums, conchs, horns, and Jai Sati Mata slogans filled the entire atmosphere. The pyre and Muktabai were quickly enveloped in massive flames. Devi Ahilya was unable to witness the event. She passed out and hit the ground. Ahilya had immense grief seeing how her daughter, Muktabai had to commit Sati. She was left with no one, even from the daughter's side of the clan. Devi, who lit up the lives of millions of people by burning her own life like a lamp; who cleared the path for her subjects to experience both physical and metaphysical pleasures; c

71 Nagrale, N. N (1979). Ahilyabai and her benevolent administration, Proceedings of the Indian History Congress Vol.40.pp 700-706. Indian History Congress retrieved on www.jstor.org/stable/44142013

CHAPTER - 3

Reform and Cultural Renaissance

A fervent devotee of Lord Shiva, her life stands as a profound testament to unwavering devotion and spirituality. She had her first meeting with Malhar Rao at the Shiv temple in her native village Chondi. Even after her marriage, when she became the daughter-in-law of the Holkar family, her religiosity accompanied her. She was even determined to become Sati after the death of her husband as per the prevailing social convention. However, she was forced to give up her resolution at the insistence of her father-in-law in favor of the subjects of the kingdom. After the incident, worship of God and service towards her subjects had become the sole objectives of her life. Service, renunciation and making donations have always been a significant part of our Sanatan (eternal) culture. The Holkars were ardent devotees of Lord Shiva. Devi Ahilya had dedicated her kingdom to Lord Shiva and ruled the kingdom as a representative of Lord Shiva. Her edicts used to be issued in the name of Lord Shiv Shankar.

This is evident from the construction and re-construction works undertaken by Devi Ahilyabai Holkar at the 12 Jyotirlingas

(Somnath,[72] Kashi Vishwanath,[73] Omkareshwar,[74] Rameshwar,[75] Mahakaleshwar,[76] and Trimbakeshwar (Maharashtra)[77]. She built many Shiva temples such as at Nasik, Kurukshetra, Ellora, Chondi and other places. In the construction of the Shiva temple at Gaya,[78] we find Devi Ahilyabai giving detailed instructions regarding the quality of the stone being quarried for the Nandi and the Assembly-hall of the temple, which must be, according to her, "strong, beautiful and first-rate." She even dedicated the personal fund of sixteen crore rupees in the service of God putting basil leaves on it.[79] With the fund, she restored the temples and places of pilgrimage throughout the country. She did not confine her services within the limits of her kingdom. Entire country was her arena, and service of humanity her object. She worked to remove the miseries of every human

---

72 Somnath (Gujarat)– One of the most sacred Jyotirlingas, Somnath was repeatedly destroyed by invaders, including Mahmud of Ghazni. Ahilyabai rebuilt the temple in the late 18th century, restoring its spiritual significance.

73 Kashi Vishwanath (Uttar Pradesh)– The famous temple in Varanasi had been demolished multiple times. Ahilyabai funded and rebuilt the temple in 1777, establishing the current structure that remains a major pilgrimage site today.

74 Omkareshwar (Madhya Pradesh)– Located on the sacred island of Mandhata, Omkareshwar Jyotirlinga was one of the most revered shrines under her rule. Ahilyabai ensured the temple was well-maintained and expanded.

75 Rameshwaram (Tamil Nadu)– This southernmost Jyotirlinga, associated with Lord Rama, was also restored under her patronage. Ahilyabai contributed to temple renovations and supported pilgrimages to this site.

76 The Mahakaleshwar Jyotirlinga in Ujjain, Madhya Pradesh, is one of the twelve Jyotirlingas, revered as a powerful and self-manifested (Swayambhu) form of Lord Shiva. This temple holds immense significance in Hinduism and has a deep historical connection with Maharani Ahilyabai Holkar (1725–1795), the ruler of Malwa.

77 Trimbakeshwar (Maharashtra)– Near Nasik, this temple is one of the holiest sites for Hindu rituals. Ahilyabai ensured its upkeep and funded its maintenance.

78 Ahilyabai funded and constructed a Shiva temple in Gaya, a sacred city for Hindus, known primarily for the Vishnupad Temple and as a center for Pind Daan (ancestral offerings). The temple was meant to serve the growing number of devotees visiting Gaya for religious rituals. The temple, built in traditional Nagara style, reflected the artistic and religious sensibilities of the time, similar to her other temple projects across India.

79 Kumar, N (2023), Lokmata Ahilyabai Holkar, Adhyayan Books.

being with a feeling of *Vasudhaiva Kutumbakam* (the whole world is a family). Her affectionate and merciful motherly heart used to melt after seeing the agony of a person, and she would make every effort within her power to remove his or her misery. Her life is a unique example of *platonic Karmyog.*[80] Rebuilding the demolished Kashi Vishwanath temple was a dream for many Maratha rulers. Yet only Rani Ahilyabai Holkar could make it a reality. Now, two and a half centuries later, her structure is in the eye of a storm. All through her life, Devi Ahilya undertook innumerable construction works throughout the country. Constructions done by her, and the services started by her in all the places of pilgrimage of the country continue till date. Devi Ahilya could not see any person in misery and in a dire condition of starving and suffering. Hence, she regularly donated food, cereals, clothes, money etc. No beggar ever returned empty-handed from her doors. On festivals, she used to distribute new clothes and food among the poor. Apart from the capital Maheshwar, special arrangements used to be made in other towns to help the poor and needy.

In the places of pilgrimage many public kitchens had been started where food and clothes used to be distributed among the poor. Devi did not want to publicize her services and win public applause. She never listed her works of charity. Hence, no authentic information is available about the places where she started charity work. But from Badrinath in the Himalayas, to Rameshwaram in the extreme South and from Jagannath Puri in the East to Dwarka and Somnath in the West, wherever we go, we find the constructions

80 Pandit S D "Ahilyabai Holkar: Reformer, Cultural Patron, and a Leader." The Sunday Guardian, n.d. Accessed on 23rd February 2025.

done and the services started by Devi Ahilya. She honored the Brahmins and savants of Vedas. She conferred state honor on many such Brahmins and donated houses, land and even villages and granted them the right to hold these properties generation after generation. She appointed those Brahmins in the temples built by her for carrying out regular worships, rituals, preachings etc. In Maheshwar as well as in other places of pilgrimage, she organized regular worship, recitation, rituals, singing of devotional songs, narration of Puranas, with thousands of Brahmins, even making arrangements for their food.

During Chaturmas, religious fervor used to be worth watching in Maheshwar. In 1781, Peshwas' counsellor Vitthal Sham Rao had written in his letter to Peshwa, "*Here in Maheshwar, religious fervor is worth watching in the month of Shravan. Daily about two to two and a half thousand Brahmins dine in public suppers. Three hundred Brahmins have been engaged in rituals, hundred in Shiva Kavach, one hundred fifty in Shiva Smarana, hundred in Surya Namaskar and hundreds of other Brahmins have been engaged in other religious activities. All these Brahmins are fed daily with delicious foods, given donations and other precious gift items.*"[81] In another letter, Vitthal Sham Rao told Peshwa, "*On the occasion of the eclipse, Devi Ahilya has donated cereals, gold and cash etc., worth rupees one lakh. She has also donated an elephant.*" In the month of Shravan, thousands of Brahmins from northern India, Gujarat, Maharashtra, and other provinces used to congregate in Maheshwar every year

81 Thakur V Vasudeo, Life and Life's work of Shree Devi Ahilya Bai Holkar , Holkar state History, printed by C.M, Shah Modern Printery Limited, Indore available on https://archive.org/details/in.ernet.dli.2015.199825/page/n5/mode/2up?view=theater accessed on September 26,2024.

to take part in the religious rituals. Devi Ahilya had made many secret donations too. At many places of pilgrimage, arrangements for the clothes of the idols of the temples, ornaments, oblation, lamps, worship, and donations, were made permanent by Devi Ahilya. For the idols of God Pandharpur,[82] Rameswaram[83] and Kashi,[84] She donated ornaments of gold and gemstones. She made permanent arrangements for carrying the holy water of the sacred Ganges from Gangotri to the forty places of pilgrimage to conduct the ceremonial bath of Shivalinga's on Maha Shivaratri[85] every year. This tradition continues until today. Descendants of the Brahmins appointed by Devi Ahilya, continue to carry out this ceremony.[86]Apart from Hinduism, Devi carried out construction work at the places of reverence for other religions also. At many places throughout the

82 Pandharpur, a sacred pilgrimage town in Maharashtra, is famous for the Vitthal-Rukmini Temple, dedicated to Lord Vitthal (a form of Lord Vishnu/Krishna). While Ahilyabai Holkar is primarily known for her devotion to Lord Shiva and the restoration of Jyotirlinga temples, she also contributed to the preservation and development of Vaishnavite pilgrimage centers, including Pandharpur.

83 During her reign, Ahilyabai undertook restoration work at the Ramanathaswamy Temple, ensuring its preservation as a major pilgrimage Centre. Funding Religious Rituals and Offerings– She supported temple rituals, making it easier for pilgrims to perform the Rameswaram Yatra, an important Hindu pilgrimage.Infrastructure for Pilgrims– She built Dharamshala (rest houses) and improved facilities for devotees traveling from distant places. Ahilyabai's efforts ensured that Rameswaram remained a thriving pilgrimage center, preserving its cultural and religious significance. Even today, pilgrims recognize her contributions, and her legacy as a protector of Hindu dharma and sacred sites continues to be celebrated.

84 Maharani Ahilyabai Holkar (1725–1795) played a historic role in rebuilding the Kashi Vishwanath Temple, ensuring its preservation after repeated destruction by invaders. Reconstruction of Kashi Vishwanath Temple (1777) – The original Kashi Vishwanath Temple was destroyed multiple times, including by Aurangzeb in the 17th century, who built the Gyan Vapi Mosque in its place. Ahilyabai Holkar rebuilt the temple in 1777, restoring its sanctity.

85 Maha Shivaratri is one of the most important Hindu festivals dedicated to Lord Shiva, the supreme deity of destruction and transformation. The name "Maha Shivaratri" means "The Great Night of Shiva," and it is observed on the 14th night of the dark fortnight (Krishna Paksha) in the month of Phalguna or Magha, depending on the regional calendar (February- March).

86 Shaivam, "Queen Devi Ahilyabai Holkar," n.d. Accessed on 1st February 2025.

country, she donated lands, estates, wealth, to the mosques, Dargahs (Moslem shrines), Maulvis and Faqirs liberally. She restored many mosques and made regular donations to several Dargahs. She not only had a sense of gratitude for the human beings but had equal love for the birds and animals. In many places, she bought fields and left them open for picking by the birds. She made arrangements for sprinkling wheat flour in the forests for the ants and flour balls daily in the rivers and ponds for the fish. Devi Ahilya had great reverence for the cows also. In every village, pastoral lands were left for the grazing by the cattle. During summer, arrangements were made to avail drinking water at different places. In winter, blankets were distributed among the needy. Devi had appointed independent employees for the purpose. All these services were run from the Devi Ahilya's personal fund. To maintain this system on a permanent basis, she had made an independent system without any support from the state exchequer. Hence, they continued in their original form despite changes of rulers after her.[87]

Tales of Devi Ahilya's munificence attracted many people towards her court. Those people told her their miseries and sought help from her. Devi Ahilya always investigated the suitability of those seekers. Once a Brahmin arrived from Kashi and told that his house was gutted in fire, and he was rendered homeless. Thus, the Brahmin requested Devi to help him financially to build his house. Devi asked the Brahmin to stay in Maheshwar for some days and arranged for his stay and food. After about a month, Devi did not give him even a single rupee. So, the Brahmin started back in dismay and reached Kashi in six months travelling via Rajasthan.

87 Indian Culture Portal. "Rajmata Ahilyabai Holkar." Indian Culture Portal, October 1, 2019.

Upon his arrival in Kashi, he discovered that his house had been fully restored by the order of Devi Ahilya. In fact, while holding the Brahmin in Maheshwar, Devi instructed her men in Kashi to check if the Brahmin was telling the truth and arranged for the restoration in case of destruction by fire. This event shows that Devi never trusted the tale of anybody without checking its authenticity.[88] Because of liberal donations, public welfare works and charitable services, Devi Ahilya was known throughout the country as Lokmata. From big kings and Nawabs to saints and sages and common people had great respect and reverence for her. During her regime, no thief or dacoit ever dared to plunder the regions run by her. Even those cereal sheds that stood amidst dense forests remained safe, because plundering these cereal sheds was considered a sin. The outlaws feared that plundering of those cereal sheds would attract the curse of pious Devi Ahilya Mata.

A Sacred Journey: A Pillar of Reform and Cultural Revival

Suffering in Ahilya's personal life was immense, there were few pieces in her heart that were stuck in old griefs. Many times, a strong urge appeared in her mind to renounce everything and stay in a place of pilgrimage and pass her remaining life in the devotion of the Lord. Nevertheless, her commitment to the kingdom and pledge she had once made to her father-in-law, late Malhar Rao stymied her from renouncing everything. She had a great reverence for the sacred Narmada River, and it was not far from Indore. There were many holy places of pilgrimage along the bank of Narmada. Devi Ahilya took a brave step and decided to

88 Jahagirdar, V (2021)., Karma Yogini: Life of Ahilyabai Holkar, translated by Sangita Soman. Mehta Publishing House

shift her capital to one such place of pilgrimage on the bank of Narmada, where she could run her kingdom as well as work towards her salvation. The best location for her capital was to be the town of Kardena in the Nimar district. She abandoned the plan to establish her capital in Kardena after the astrologers informed her that the village was unsuitable for serving as the capital. After that, she noticed Maheshwar. She saw Maheshwar as the best location for both fulfilling her religious craving and building the capital. Devi Ahilya's establishment of the capital at Maheshwar was advantageous for the area. Devi Ahilya lived in Maheshwar for roughly twenty-eight years of her life. Maheshwar emerged as a major hub at this time and gained significance on the national map.[89] Frequent visits from rulers, ambassadors, savants, sages, and ascetics from all the nation's major provinces and the state even experienced a complete transformation and was once again regarded as one of India's major cities.[90]

Renowned in ancient India as Avantika[91] and Mahishmati,[92] Ujjain of Malwa and Maheshwar of Nimar are the two prominent places of pilgrimage with great historical

---

89 Indian Culture Portal. "Rajmata Ahilyabai Holkar." Indian Culture Portal, October 1, 2019.

90 Thakur V Vasudeo, Life and Life's work of Shree Devi Ahilya Bai Holkar , Holkar state History, printed by C.M, Shah Modern Printery Limited, Indore available on https://archive.org/details/in.ernet.dli.2015.199825/page/n5/mode/2up?view=theater accessed on September 26,2024.

91 Avantika refers to Ujjain, an ancient and historically significant city in the Malwa region of Madhya Pradesh, India. Ujjain was known as Avantika in ancient times and was a major center of learning, trade, and spirituality. It is one of the seven Moksha-puris (sacred cities) in Hinduism and is famous for the Mahakaleshwar Jyotirlinga, one of the twelve Jyotirlingas of Lord Shiva.

92 Mahishmati refers to Maheshwar, a town in the Nimar region of Madhya Pradesh. In ancient times, Maheshwar was known as Mahishmati and was a significant kingdom mentioned in Hindu scriptures like the Mahabharata and Puranas. It was once the capital of the legendary King Kartavirya Arjuna (Sahasrarjuna). Later, in the 18th century, it became famous as the seat of Maharani Ahilyabai Holkar, who revitalized the town and built many temples and ghats along the Narmada River.

significance situated near Indore. Both these cities have great archaeological importance and find mention in the scriptures of Jain and Buddhist besides great epics like Ramayana and Mahabharata and many Puranas. Since Maheshwar was situated within the Holkar Kingdom, Devi Ahilya selected this place to build her capital. It had been a prosperous and flourishing city during the ages of Ramayana and Mahabharata. Evidence shows that Arjuna had arrived here during his mission of universal conquest. Narmada is one of India's seven most prominent and sacred rivers. It is the only river in the world which is circulated by thousands of devotees every year. Devi Ahilya too had strong faith and reverence for Narmada. Thus, she built her capital in Maheshwar and spent a major part of her life near the bank of Narmada. In Maheshwar, Ahilyabai got the renovation of many old temples done, which were on the verge of ruins. She also got many new temples and embankments as well as many houses built for the savants, Brahmins, and weavers. After becoming the capital of Devi Ahilya's kingdom, its political, social as well as commercial importance of Maheshwar also grew significantly.[93] Devi Ahilya invited selected religious teachers, astrologers, puranic psalmists, artists, and artisans from all over the country and helped them to settle in Maheshwar. She also started many Sanskrit schools. Tradition of regular worship and other religious ceremonies in the temples also began in her time. To conduct these functions, hundreds of Brahmins and priests also settled in Maheshwar.[94] Recitation of hymns and musical sounds

93 Chandrasekhar, M, Yugandhara Ahilyabai Holkar: Historical Novel Focusing on The Inspiring Life of Devi Ahilya Bai Holkar, New Delhi: Prabhat Prakashan Pvt. Ltd., 2024.

94 Khadpekar, V(2024), Dnyat Ani Adnyat: Ahilyabai Holkar (Lokavrutti), Mumbai: Rajhans Prakashan.

of songs, conchs and other instruments reverberated all day long in the temples of Maheshwar. Devi Ahilya opened her treasure to make donations to the Brahmins and the poor and to feed them public kitchens used to be run by her aid.

Devi Ahilya also got the construction of temples, embankments, inns, canopies done in almost all the places of pilgrimage in the entire country. Construction of these structures required thousands of artisans and masons. Thousands of sculptors, statuaries, artisans who were searching for employment, came to settle in Maheshwar. Efforts of Devi Ahilya led to the establishment of Maheshwar as a prominent center of cloth industry on the commercial map of the country. She invited the skilled weavers from all parts of the country and helped them to settle in Maheshwar. She helped them financially to start their business, she also bought sarees and other goods produced by those weavers to encourage them. Because of her inspiration and incentives, high quality sarees and clothes began to be produced in Maheshwar. These products had exquisite artistic work also. Devi Ahilya herself used to wear sarees manufactured in Maheshwar and presented her guests with the clothes made in Maheshwar, as gifts. Business of the weavers began to flourish because of the liberal support, high taste and incentives of Devi Ahilya and the artisans also grew in prosperity.[95] Ahilyabai fosters her subjects like her own children. She takes full care of their safety and comfort. She pledged to distribute free food daily through the public kitchens for the poor. From the description, it becomes clear how a small, ordinary town Maheshwar transformed into a flourishing city through her efforts. Being the capital of Holkar Kingdom, many kings sent their representatives to

95 Jahagirdar, V(2021), Karma Yogini: Life of Ahilyabai Holkar, Pune: Mehta Publishing House.

stay permanently in Maheshwar.[96]

Despite the flourishing capital Devi Ahilya stayed in her simple residence and could aptly be called a hermitage. It appeared more like a place of pilgrimage, having a divinely tranquil ambience. In one of the rooms, Devi had fenced off some place for worship, where every morning she prayed and worshipped God. In the courtyard of the house, there was a small Tulsi-grove, and in front of the house was the huge embankment of Narmada. Near the house there was a small garden in which flowers and Tulsi plants had been grown for the purpose of worship. It is still maintained in the same state as it used to be at the time of Devi Ahilya. Thousands of people from all over the world visit Maheshwar to pay their tribute to Devi Ahilya even today. When they return, they take great inspiration from her brilliant life and work with them. After watching this simple residence of Devi Ahilya and while presiding over the function of Devi Ahilya National Award ceremony in Indore, Governor of Madhya Pradesh, His Highness Dr. Bhai Mahaveer said in his speech, "*People, particularly the politicians must visit Maheshwar and see the simple but extraordinary residence of Devi Ahilya. Only then, they will realize how, despite being the owner of a huge and prosperous kingdom, the pious Devi Ahilya spent her life like an expiator. Having seen her lifestyle, the modern politicians will be ashamed of their luxurious life.*"[97]

---

96 Thakur V Vasudeo, Life and Life's work of Shree Devi Ahilya Bai Holkar , Holkar state History, printed by C.M, Shah Modern Printery Limited, Indore available on https://archive.org/details/in.ernet.dli.2015.199825/page/n5/mode/2up?view=theater accessed on September 26,2024.

97 Thakur V Vasudeo, Life and Life's-work of Shree Devi Ahilya Bai Holkar , Holkar state History, printed by C.M, Shah Modern Printery Limited, Indore available on https://archive.org/details/in.ernet.dli.2015.199825/page/n5/mode/2up?view=theater accessed on October 26,2024.

Guardian of Faith: Her Contributions to Religious Architecture

The Holkar family never used public funds to meet their personal and family expenses. Founder of the Holkar Kingdom, Malhar Rao Holkar had received, upon request to Shrimant Peshwa, some properties in the name of his wife Gautamabai to meet the personal expenses of his family. The Queen consort had the right to look after this personal property. Apart from the revenue generated from this property, property and precious items received by the Queen as gifts also used to be deposited in the personal fund. Devi Ahilya inherited the personal fund, which at that time contained about sixteen crore rupees. After the death of her only son Maley Rao, Devi Ahilya decided to use the property of personal fund in charitable works. During the time of late Malhar Rao, Devi Ahilya had got ample opportunities to tour the various places of pilgrimage. She was thus fully aware that the expenses that are incurred for carrying out pilgrimage tours, outstation stay, and feeding were beyond the reach of the poor pilgrims.[98]

Those days, most of the places of pilgrimage lacked the proper facilities for staying and dining at affordable rates. Moreover, most parts of the country were under the rule of the invaders. Hence, most of the temples and Ghats in the places of Hindus' pilgrimage were in miserable conditions. Devi Ahilya decided to spend the property of her personal fund in the renovation of these structures. Apart from the construction of Ghats on the rivers throughout India,

98 Baillie Joanna Ahilya Bai Holkar: One of the Least Known Indian Social Reformers, International Journal of Research, March 26, 2022 accessed on https://internationaljournalofresearch.com/2022/03/26/ahilya-bai-holkar-one-of-the-least-known-indian-social-reformer/

renovations and restoration of the temples demolished by the foreign invaders, digging of wells, stepwells and sumps and construction of new temples took place. Devi Ahilya planned a free public kitchen to feed the poor and the pilgrims. For the realization of her plan, she conducted lengthy discussions with the sages and saints and the pilgrims, who had visited various places of pilgrimage, to comprehend the problems and necessities of these places. After immersive deliberations, she drew a comprehensive plan to carry out the construction works. She wrote letters to all the kings of the country and requested them to send their skilled sculptors and artisans and appointed them for the construction works. Structures built by Devi Ahilya are visible in the uncountable places of pilgrimage across the length and breadth of India including Himalayas. From Badrinath and Kedarnath in the North to Rameshwaram in extreme South, and from Jagannath Puri in the East to Dwarka, Somnath in the West there is not even a single place of pilgrimage, which does not have a piece of sculpture and architecture built by Devi Ahilya. Devi Ahilya did not consider the construction of temples and other structures as an end to her duty. For the maintenance of the structures built by her, she had arranged for a separate fund. Devi understood well that all the buildings that she built, would soon turn into ruins if she did not arrange for their maintenance. She had seen the dilapidated condition of the structures built by preceding rulers.[99] Hence, Devi appointed many able and skilled professionals for the maintenance of the structures and made stable arrangements to fulfil their

99 Diwan, H. D., Sharma, A., Bhaduria, S. S., Kadwe, P., Sanyal, D., & Sharma, J. (2020). Ancient Hindu rock monuments, configuration and architectural features of Ahilya Devi Fort of Holkar Dynasty, Mahismati Region, Maheshwar, Narmada Valley, Central India. *International Journal of Scientific Development and Research*, *5*(11), 134. Retrieved from https://www.ijsdr.org/

financial requirements. Hence, even three hundred years after the death of Devi Ahilya, structures built by her and the services that she constructed and renovated are still visible at every place of pilgrimage. They are exquisite examples of artistic work. All of them are excellent examples of Indian architecture. For the construction of the temples, Devi Ahilya had purchased the lands and transferred them to temple trusts. She had also appointed the priests, psalmists, preachers and religious savants and managers for the temples and had fixed their salaries from the state funds.[100] She also arranged annual grants for the maintenance of these temples. Devi Ahilya was a fervent devotee of Lord Shiva. Hence, she got the maximum number of Shiva temples built. But she did not ignore other sects either. She got many temples of other deities built and restored. Evidence was also available that supports the fact that Devi had issued grants for the religious places of other religions also like mosques and Dargah (shrines) etc. Mughal Emperor Aurangzeb had demolished the famous Kashi Vishwanath temple in 1667. Devi Ahilya got this temple rebuilt in 1785.[101] She got a 51 feet high temple as well as Jagmohan and Chakrapani temples built in Varanasi. She also got the restoration of old Ghats done and embankments built. She also got a road constructed from Calcutta to Kashi. Famous Somnath temple, which had been demolished by Mahmud of Ghazni, was restored to a new imposing structure by Devi Ahilya.

100 Nath, R(1995), Indore: The City of Ahilyabai Holkar (Jaipur: Historical Research Documentation Programme,).

101 Sharma, J.N(1988)., Ahilyabai Holkar: The Philosopher Queen, Indore: Malwa Prakashan.

Ancient Saptapuri,[102] twelve Jyotirlingas and Char Dhama (four pilgrimage)[103] are considered as the major places of pilgrimage in Hinduism. In all these places, Devi made proper arrangements for bathing, worshipping, prayers, staying and dining of the pilgrims. She established an ideal example of dedicated service. In the regime of Devi Ahilya, sculptures and artisans remained engaged continuously for thirty years in different parts of the country. Devi used to say, "*This Holkar chisel must work continuously. Construction work must never be stopped.*"[104] And indeed, chisels and hammers of Devi continued to work relentlessly, examples of which are present throughout the country. One can imagine the inaccessibility of pilgrimages like Badrinath, Kedarnath and Gangotri two hundred and fifty years ago. These places of pilgrimage remain inaccessible until today. But Devi had no word like impossible in her lexicon, nor did she allow anybody to make excuses. In his book *Memories of Central India*, Sir Malcom writes that his associate, Capt. D.T. Stuart managed to reach Kedarnath in 1818, facing many hurdles in the way. He was amazed to see that even in that inaccessible

---

102 The Saptapuri are the seven most sacred pilgrimage cities in Hinduism. These cities are believed to grant moksha (liberation) to those who visit them with devotion. Each city has deep mythological, historical, and religious significance. Kashi (Varanasi, Uttar Pradesh), Ayodhya (Uttar Pradesh), Mathura (Uttar Pradesh) Haridwar (Uttarakhand) Kanchipuram (Tamil Nadu) Ujjain (Madhya Pradesh) and Dwarka (Gujarat).

103 The Char Dham refers to the four most important pilgrimage sites in Hinduism, believed to be the pathway to moksha (liberation). These four sites are spread across different corners of India and are associated with Lord Vishnu and his incarnations. These are Badrinath (Uttarakhand) – Dedicated to Lord Vishnu (Badri Narayan), located in the Himalayas, Dwarka (Gujarat)– The ancient kingdom of Lord Krishna, on the western coast, Puri (Odisha)– Home to Jagannath Temple, an important site for Vaishnavism and Rameswaram (Tamil Nadu)– A sacred Shaiva-Vaishnava pilgrimage site, linked to Lord Rama's worship of Shiva.

104 Pandit Shanti Shree, Ahilyabai Holkar: Reformer, Cultural Patron, and a Leader." The Sunday Guardian, n.d. Accessed on 23rd February 2025.https://sundayguardianlive.com/opinion/ahilyabai-holkar-reformer-cultural-patron-and-a-leader#google_vignette

remote place hospice and sump were present, which were built by Devi Ahilya. He also saw the public kitchen that served twenty-four hours a day run by Devi Ahilya in Giri Tirth of Dev Prayag.[105]

Devi Ahilya had built her capital in Maheshwar. There she had got a huge embankment built on Narmada. Perhaps no other river in the world has such a huge jetty. For her own residence, Devi built a house at such a place from where she could easily see the religious activities taking place on the banks of Narmada. From the grove of Tulsi in the courtyard of her residence, the entire sacred ambience of Narmada bank was visible. Sir Malcom describes the Siddhanath temple which was built by Devi Ahilya, 'as the excellent temple architecture in Central India. At the same spot in Alampur, where her father-in-law, late Malhar Rao Holkar had breathed his last, Devi got a huge canopy-cum-ccnotaph and a Harihareshwar temple[106] built. Both these structures are exquisite pieces of architecture. At the place of her birth Chondi, Devi Ahilya got a temple, and a jetty built on the river. Two hundred and fifty years ago, means of transport were limited in the country. Travelling from one place to another would require too much time. Besides there were every kind of danger lurking on the way, transportation of building materials was even more troublesome. Despite all the difficulties, construction works carried out by Devi

105 Diwan, H. D., Sharma, A., Bhaduria, S. S., Kadwe, P., Sanyal, D., & Sharma, J. (2020). Ancient Hindu rock monuments, configuration and architectural features of Ahilya Devi Fort of Holkar Dynasty, Mahismati Region, Maheshwar, Narmada Valley, Central India. *International Journal of Scientific Development and Research*, *5*(11), 134. Retrieved from https://www.ijsdr.org/

106 The Harihareshwar Temple, built by Devi Ahilyabai Holkar, is a significant temple dedicated to Harihara, a combined form of Lord Vishnu (Hari) and Lord Shiva (Hara). This temple represents the unity of Shaivism and Vaishnavism, two major traditions in Hinduism.

Ahilya throughout the country still remains unparalleled and amazing.

Devi Ahilya used to appoint the workers and the artisan for the construction works only after proper scrutiny. She also kept close watch on their work. Squandering, carelessness, and corruption were unbearable to her. She took no time in removing such people from work. During a construction work in Nasik, when she came to know about unnecessary delay and forgery in funds by a man, she immediately removed him from work. Similarly, she was suspicious about the strength of Shri Ram temple in Pandharpur. She, therefore, got the strength of the temple tested by making an elephant walk on its roof in her presence. Only after getting fully satisfied, she made the payment for the construction. Every year on the Ekadashi (eleventh day) of Asadh and Kartik months, thousands of people visit walking. They used to have a sight of Lord Vitthal in Pandharpur.[107] For their ease, Devi Ahilya bought the agriculture rights in the surrounding forests, and got many stepwells and sumps dug on these lands and leased out the fields to the farmers for tilling on hereditary basis. She also made these farmers responsible for freely feeding the pilgrims with Jhunaka Bhakar (gram flour breads) and drinking water. At many other places in the country, Devi provided the people with land and cattle and made them responsible for offering free milk to the pilgrims. Descendants of these families remember these things with pride and express their gratitude to Devi Ahilya. On the way to Omkareshwar and many other places of pilgrimage, Devi

107 Diwan, H. D., Sharma, A., Bhadauria, S. S., Kadwe, P., Sanyal, D., & Sharma, J. (2020). Ancient Hindu rock monuments, configuration and architectural features of Ahilya Devi Fort of Holkar Dynasty, Mahismati Region, Maheshwar, Narmada Valley, Central India. *International Journal of Scientific Development and Research*, *5*(11), 134. Retrieved from https://www.ijsdr.org/

Ahilya had built many beautiful and artistic stepwells; many of which are quenching the thirst of the pilgrims even today. Through her construction works she played an important role in raising a sense of devotion among the people for these places of pilgrimage.

CHAPTER - 4

Queenship and Governance : Political Empowerment

Ahilyabai Holkar was a visionary and a true leader who created an ideal welfare state which was people centric. During those days, Traditional succession laws barred women from ascending to the throne, restricting royal inheritance to male heirs. Upon a ruler's death, only sons were eligible to contest the throne, thereby excluding women from succession. Still, there are several examples of women, ruling within the Maratha polity. Tara Bai[108] serves as a notable example, having spearheaded the resistance against Mughal forces in the early eighteenth century and maintaining significant political influence for subsequent decades. Her example demonstrates how women could exercise actual authority either as wives (or widows) or as mothers (and regents) to potential heirs. Successful female governance required exceptional capability, determination, and favorable conditions. For Ahilyabai, these circumstances emerged following her husband's battlefield death in 1754, leaving her with a young son. Thereafter, the father-in-law, the great general Malhar Rao Holkar, seems to have trained her both in

108 Seshan (2014) The Maratha State: Some Preliminary Considerations. Indian Historical Review, 41, no.1 35-46.

military affairs and administration. Several letters from Malhar Rao Holkar to Ahilyabai show that she was (besides being literate) fully involved in military and diplomatic activities well before her father-in law's death. [109]

Letters of Malhar Rao to Devi Ahilya

In a letter in 1765, he wrote her the following instructions, "Proceed to Gwalior after crossing the Chambal. You may halt there for four or five days. You should keep your big artillery and arrange for its ammunition as much as possible. The big artillery should be kept at Gwalior, and you should proceed further after making proper arrangements for its expenses for a month. On the march you should arrange for military posts to be located for the protection of the road." Malhar Rao assumed that she was competent to handle both civil and military affairs and occasionally favored her with overall military advice: "Whenever you reduce a fortress of the Gohad chief, send an adequate amount of artillery. In no case should you be entrenched before a fort. As far as possible get the object by means of prestige."[110]Several weeks after Ahilyabai's arrival in Indore, he recommended her to manage the administration of two eastern Malwa districts, confident in her capabilities.[111] Following Malhar

---

109 Thakur V Vasudeo, Life and Life's-work of Shree Devi Ahilya Bai Holkar , Holkar state History, printed by C.M,Shah Modern Printery Limited, Indore available on https://archive.org/details/in.ernet.dli.2015.199825/page/n5/mode/2up?view=theater accessed on October 26,2024.

110 Burway, M. W (1925) Life of His Highness Maharaja Tukoji Rao Holkar II, GCSI, Ruler of Indore (1835-1886)

111 Diwan, H. D., Sharma, A., Bhadauria, S. S., Kadwe, P., Sanyal, D., & Sharma, J. (2020). Ancient Hindu rock monuments, configuration and architectural features of Ahilya Devi Fort of Holkar Dynasty, Mahismati Region, Maheshwar, Narmada Valley, Central India. *International Journal of Scientific Development and Research*, *5*(11), 134. Retrieved from https://www.ijsdr.org/

Rao's death and the subsequent passing of Ahilyabai's son (the rightful heir) who suffered from mental breakdown and died within a year of succession, she, at thirty years of age, had already demonstrated her prowess in both military and administrative matters. Instead of choosing to adopt an heir, she submitted a petition to the Peshwa requesting direct control of the Holkar territories. She stood ready to command her forces against the opposing faction within the central government, but the matter was ultimately resolved when the Peshwa sent a letter confirming her authority. In a novel and ingenious solution, she chose Tukoji Holkar, commander of the "household" troops (but no relative), to head all military aspects of her rule. The equilibrium in power-sharing endured for thirty years, until both passed away in the 1790s. Ahilyabai focused on fair governance, maintaining peace, and fostering economic growth within the Holkar territories, with particular emphasis on Malwa.

Inclusive Governance and Policy

Her primary approach to governance was characterized by reasonable taxation and a profound respect for the established rights of village officials and landowners.[112] She personally attended to all grievances, and whilst regularly directing cases to equity courts, arbitration panels and her ministers for resolution, she remained consistently approachable. Her commitment to justice was notably strong, and historical accounts indicate her patience and dedication in addressing even minor disputes when brought before her for judgement. Throughout her thirty-year reign, Ahilyabai demonstrated

112 Javlekar, A, Lokmata Ahilyabai (2002): Arvind Javlekar's Account of an Inspirational Queen and Philanthropist (New Delhi: Prabhat Prakashan.

exceptional diplomatic and administrative capabilities, as evidenced by the fact that her territories in Malwa remained unaffected by conflicts from neighboring armed groups, despite ongoing wars in both northern and southern regions. Her governance was rooted in civilization ethos of *Samajik Samrasta*[113] which represents a philosophical vision that transcends the conventional confines of social justice. It is not merely a response to social disparities, but a dynamic and continuous process aimed at fostering an equitable society where every segment of the community is provided with dignified means to participate and thrive. Rather than focusing solely on redistributive justice, *Samajik Samrasta* aspires to create a society where harmony and inclusion are deeply ingrained in the social fabric. The concept states that *Samata* (equity), meaning to ensuring fair resource allocation; *Mamata* (dignity), acknowledging each person's inherent worth; *Ramata* (sincerity), community relations; *Samanata* (equality), supporting universal rights and opportunities; and Tartamyata (continuity), consistent dedication to these principles. She followed these principles in her work with disadvantaged groups, specifically the Bhils, Gonds, and Dalits. Her approach involved direct community engagement, creation of economic prospects, and elimination of social barriers, thus establishing a framework for an all-encompassing society. Her administrative strategy helped these communities from being excluded groups into becoming active members in the

113 Paswan A N https://indianexpress.com/article/opinion/columns/how-savarkar-fought-for-a-casteless-society-7794728/. Accessed on January 2nd, 2025

social and economic activities[114]. Samajik Samarasta offers a framework that incorporates fairness, respect, authenticity, equality, and persistence. This outlook envisions a society where all individuals receive recognition and empowerment. Ahilyabai's administration successfully halted the attacks from Bhils and Gonds, the hill tribes who had previously targeted agricultural settlements. Her governance was characterized by reforms aimed at improving the conditions of the Bhils, Gonds and other underprivileged tribal groups. She recognized these communities as vital components of society and launched comprehensive policies to better their socio-economic conditions. She chose inclusion rather than isolation and instead of excluding tribal groups who had participated in plundering activities, she instead established direct communication channels with them.

Through diplomatic discussions, she convinced these communities to abandon their unlawful pursuits. Additionally, she introduced a structured taxation system that required locals to pay for utilizing forest resources owned by tribal communities. This arrangement ensured that tribes received proper compensation for their natural resources. This dual-purpose strategy effectively reduced criminal activities while simultaneously empowering tribal communities by integrating them into the broader economic framework. Through her policies, she successfully stopped raids by offering employment alternatives to these tribal communities and because of these initiatives both tribal and other marginalized communities were able to transition from

114 Thakur V Vasudeo, Life and Life's work of Shree Devi Ahilya Bai Holkar , Holkar state History, printed by C.M, Shah Modern Printery Limited, Indore available on https://archive.org/details/in.ernet.dli.2015.199825/page/n5/mode/2up?view=theater accessed on September 26,2024.

marginalization to life of dignity. By creating employment opportunities for both tribal groups and the marginalized. Ahilyabai implemented progressive policies that gave way for opportunities for disadvantaged groups across social, financial, and educational spheres. She helped tribal populations to transition from their nomadic existence and forest-based sustenance to settled farming practices. All these measured led to their social cohesion and steadier livelihoods. In the textile sector, she gave employments to marginalized and put in place skill development programs for them. The focus on education and industrial training helped these communities progress. Virtually all ministers and officials remained in their positions throughout her rule, an example of stability during her reign. She developed Indore from a basic settlement into a prosperous and sophisticated urban center. In the period of Malcolm (the 1830s and 1840s), she gained an enduring reputation, which continues today, for her unequivocal defense of widows' rights to retain their late husbands' properties, protecting them from appropriation by the state and greedy relatives. The infrastructural evidence of her excellent governance can be seen through the fortifications and transport routes in Malwa, along with various religious institutions (encompassing temples, dharmshalas, water tanks, bathing ghats and comparable facilities) within Malwa and at distant sacred sites including Varanasi, Dwarka in Gujarat, Rameshwaram and Gaya. She supported religious celebrations and contributed towards maintaining regular worship practices at numerous Hindu temples. In contemporary Malwa, she is regarded as a holy figure, reflecting the lasting influence of her ethical and accountable administration.

Her assertion as a 'just' ruler: Correspondence with Tukoji [115]

When Tukoji presented Devi with an unsanctioned bill for war expenses and proposed that the Sardars should cover the costs, she responded firmly. In her written reply, she emphasized that it would be unfair to burden the Sardars with these payments. She explained that their allotments were strictly calculated based on the number of servicemen under their command, without any excess, and pointed out that the Sardars were actively serving in the field at that time.

"*Hence it is not justified under the circumstances to ask them to pay,*" she wrote. [116]

In a correspondence, Tukoji, the commander-in-chief of the Holkar forces, communicated his lack of significant accomplishments in the Deccan and requested financial support to execute a major campaign as per the Peshwa's wishes. Ahilya Bai's response was direct: "From where the money will come. You say that the receipts from the Swadesh territory (Southern) have already been paid to the Poona treasury. You were on the spot, and nothing has been achieved. This is not fair."[117] She admonished Tukoji by referencing her father-in-law's philosophy of addressing issues promptly, regardless of their nature, without waiting for external support or directives. She criticized his delayed strategic planning, stating, "The schemes of campaign

115 Burway, M. W. (1925). Life of His Highness Maharaja Tukoji Rao Holkar II, GCSI, Ruler of Indore (1835-1886). Holkar State Printing Press, Indore retrieved from https://archive.org/details/dli.ministry.03869/page/n9/mode/2up accessed on 17th September 2024.

116 Zelliott, E. (2001). Ahilyabai Holkar: A Magnificent Ruler, Saintly Administrator, May-June 2001 issue of Manushi

117 Kumar, N (2023) Lokmata Ahilyabai Holkar, Adhyayan Books

are being planned (by you) when the clouds have already appeared in the sky! How can artillery and other war material reach you in the rains?"[118] Her communication style remained composed and rational, consistently supported by logical arguments. Her virtuous character, unwavering integrity, commitment to fairness and justice, coupled with her spiritual devotion and moral strength, commanded respect and obedience from others. She demonstrated genuine concern for the rights of all her subjects, regardless of their social standing. She declined suggestions, stating "...memoranda for future working of the Parganas is being sent to you ... You should not, henceforth no wise, interfere with affairs of Mamlat of the Pargana ... Please consult the officials first."[119]

Her governance model was people centric, and she ensured the wellbeing of all citizens irrespective of caste and class, and under her astute leadership and firm governance, the state experienced unprecedented peace and prosperity. Her reign was marked by peace and plenty, an absence of famine, social harmony, and a contented populace and officials. The Saranjami Sardars, who were bound to maintain the prescribed number of cavalries, formed the "Huzrut" or the standing army.[120] Tukoji, the Subedar, who represented the military aspect of Devi Ahilya Bai's administration, remained most respectful and loyal towards her. In a letter, he expressed his sincere regret for going astray and requested

118 Burway, M.W(1925)., Life of His Highness Maharaja Tukoji Rao Holkar II, GCSI, Ruler of Indore (1835–1886).

119 Jahagirdar, V (2020) Karma Yogini: Life of Ahilyabai Holkar Mehta Publishing House

120 Joshi, G. K (1978), Ahilyabai Holkar (Jivan Charitra) Book Source: Digital Library of India Item 2015.308798 retrieved from https://archive.org/details/in.ernet.dli.2015.308798/page/n19/mode/2up

that he and his entire family live under Devi Ahilya Bai's orders. In another letter, he requested Dev to bring his son to his senses. When Ahilya Bai was deeply upset by her daughter Mukta Bai becoming a sati in 1791, Tukoji Holkar made an earnest appeal to her, "" Until I come there, please do not think of going anywhere out; if you do, I again swear by the feet of the late revered Subedar (Malhar Rao), and on my life." She organized a good postal system, and all soldiers and subjects had faith that in case of their death in the field or unprovoked violence, their family would be taken care of by the Devi.[121]Ahilya Bai's rule is known for peace and tranquility and for "trophies of peace and not war" in that turbulent period where there were wars, political instability, sieges, and conflicts in neighboring regions. The only strife and struggle during her 30 years reign was the Rampura affair, which also brought to light both her brilliance at diplomacy and statesmanship. As V.V. Thakur writes, "Peace was her policy in the main, when opposed she first tried reconciliation. When that failed, recourse to arms was the next but necessary step. Stronger measures foreign to her nature when necessitated, and she faltered not. But at last, all was forgotten and forgiven. An opportunity for repentance and reform was offered and the whole affair ended in "Justice mingled with mercy."" [122] There are many instances which support this assessment of the great lady who was venerated as a most pious and saintly, a mother-

121 Burway, M. W. (1925). Life of His Highness Maharaja Tukoji Rao Holkar II, GCSI, Ruler of Indore (1835-1886). Holkar State Printing Press, Indore retrieved from https://archive.org/details/dli.ministry.03869/page/n9/mode/2up accessed on 17th September 2024.

122 Thakur V Vasudeo, Life and Life's-work of Shree Devi Ahilya Bai Holkar , Holkar state History, printed by C.M,Shah Modern Printery Limited, Indore available on https://archive.org/details/in.ernet.dli.2015.199825/page/n5/mode/2up?view=theater accessed on October 26,2024.

like figure during her lifetime. In that period of instability and turbulence Ahilya Bai had one of the most stable reigns of the 18th Century so much so that her territories in Malwa were never attacked or disrupted by local battles during her reign in spite of wars all around.

Strategic Wisdom and Architectural Legacy

Ahilyabai Holkar laid great emphasis on architectural development which played a pivotal role in her success as a ruler. Unlike many leaders who relied on fear and coercion to command respect, Ahilyabai earned the admiration and loyalty of her people through a deep understanding of their needs and desires. By commissioning the construction of religious structures, temples, and public works, she provided her subjects with tangible symbols of prosperity, faith, and care. These architectural wonders were not merely tools of political control but expressions of her commitment to the well-being of her kingdom.[123] Her approach was rooted in a sense of inclusivity and respect for her people's spiritual and cultural practices, which fostered a genuine sense of devotion and reverence. Her emphasis on building places of worship, rest houses, and other communal spaces demonstrated a leader who prioritized the welfare of her subjects over personal glory. This thoughtful and compassionate approach to governance helped her cultivate lasting respect and affection, establishing her as a ruler who was loved and revered, rather than feared.

During the 18th century, under the rulership of the Peshwas,

123 Burway, M. W. (1925). Life of His Highness Maharaja Tukoji Rao Holkar II, GCSI, Ruler of Indore (1835-1886). Holkar State Printing Press, Indore retrieved from https://archive.org/details/dli.ministry.03869/page/n9/mode/2up accessed on 17th September 2024.

the power of the Maratha polity (1674-1818) expanded greatly from its Maharashtrian homeland. When the Mughal emperor Aurangzeb died in 1707, the resulting fragmentation and weakness of the Mughal Empire spurred the Maratha Prime Minister, Balaji Bajirao, to push the Marathas northward into Malwa and beyond.[124] Few Maratha families rose to prominence in Bajirao's military campaigns, including the Holkars, the Scandia's, and the Gaekwads. As the century unfolded, these Maratha families experienced a great deal of social mobility; their domains enlarged, and the power they wielded expanded rapidly. Ahilyabai Holkar became the ruling queen of Holkar territory in 1767. She quickly emerged as one of the most extraordinary leaders of 18th century India. During her father-in-law's reign, Ahilyabai was deeply involved in military and diplomatic activities, and after his death was followed by that of her own son, Ahilyabai attained the right to take over the administration of Holkar territory.

During her subsequent 30-year reign she justly administered the Holkar kingdom and brought great prosperity to it. She was more successful than any previous ruler in halting devastating raids by local hill tribes, and she developed Indore into a prosperous and beautiful city.[125] She was also the most active architectural patron of any in the Maratha confederacy.

She established fortifications and constructed roadways throughout Malwa, whilst also setting up numerous religious

124 Joshi, G.K (1978) Ahilyabai Holkar (Jivan Charitra). Book Source: Digital Library of India Item 2015.308798

125 Burway, M. W. (1925). Life of His Highness Maharaja Tukoji Rao Holkar II, GCSI, Ruler of Indore (1835-1886). Holkar State Printing Press, Indore retrieved from https://archive.org/details/dli.ministry.03869/page/n9/mode/2up accessed on 17th September 2024.

foundations across central and northern regions of India. These included places of worship, travelers' shelters, water reservoirs and ghats. Additionally, she provided financial support for religious celebrations and contributed regular donations to sustain worship activities in various Hindu temples. Notwithstanding her renowned status during her life and the reverence she garnered in Maharashtra and Malwa, along with her extensive architectural contributions, minimal research exists on the religious structures she established. The two chhatris built under Ahilyabai's commission to honor her late father-in-law, Malhar Rao, deserve attention. Further examination is required to understand her sponsorship of four jyotirlinga temples, situated at various locations across northern and central India. A collection of twelve jyotirlingas, where the Hindu deity Shiva is venerated in the form of self-manifested linga (Shiva's non-anthropomorphic, phallic symbol) of divine light, was established during the tenth to eleventh centuries.[126] This establishment was part of an initiative to implement Saivism throughout India. These jyotirlingas and their temple structures are distributed across India's vast geography, spanning from Tamil Nadu in the south to Uttarakhand in the north, from Varanasi in the east to Somanath in Gujarat in the west, effectively transforming the Indian terrain into a sacred Saivite geometric pattern. Most of the recognized jyotirlinga temples have early medieval foundations and were likely important local Saivite temples before being integrated into the codified, pan-Indian set of twelve.

By the 13th and 14th centuries, there is evidence of extensive additional building activities at multiple jyotirlinga sites. In

126 MAP Academy. "Ahilyabai Holkar." Glossary entry. Accessed on December 12th, 2024.

the 18th century under the Marathas rebuilding or renovating jyotirlinga temples was once again a significant activity, and pilgrimage to jyotirlinga temples was encouraged. Of the 12 classified jyotirlinga sites, seven received elite Maratha patronage in the 18th century, including four temples rebuilt or substantially renovated by Ahilyabai:

- The Vaidyanath (Baijnath) Temple, Parli, Maharashtra, rebuilt upon existing Yadava foundations in 1776.[127]
- The Vishwanath Temple, Varanasi, Uttar Pradesh, built at a site adjacent to an earlier Vishwanath Temple (inside Gyan Vapi) in 1777.[128]
- The Ghrineśvara Temple, Ellora, Maharashtra, rebuilt on existing Yadava foundations in the 1780s.[129]
- The Somanath Temple, Saurashtra, Gujarat, built at a site adjacent to the original in 1783 or 1785.[130]

As Belli Bose has suggested, we can perceive in Ahilyabai's architectural patronage a desire to legitimize her authority

127 The Vaidyanath Temple in Parli, Maharashtra, is a revered site among the twelve Jyotirlingas. While the exact date of its original construction is unclear, it is believed to have been built during the Yadava period, which dates to the 12th or 13th century. The temple was rebuilt upon its existing foundations by Rani Ahilyabai Holkar in the 1700s,

128 The Vishvanatha Temple in Varanasi, Uttar Pradesh, was rebuilt adjacent to the earlier Vishvanatha Temple site. Originally constructed in 1490, it was destroyed by Aurangzeb in 1669 and rebuilt by Ahilyabai Holkar in 1780. The temple is a significant Hindu pilgrimage site, symbolizing spiritual resilience and devotion

129 The Ghrineśvara Temple, located near Ellora in Maharashtra, is often confused with the Kailasa Temple, another prominent site in the region. However, the Ghrineśvara Temple is distinct and is known for its historical significance. The Ghrineśvara Temple, located near Ellora in Maharashtra, is often confused with the Kailasa Temple, another prominent site in the region. However, the Ghrineśvara Temple is distinct and is known for its historical significance.

130 The Somnath Temple in Saurashtra, Gujarat, has a complex history of destruction and rebuilding. In 1783, Ahilyabai Holkar of the Holkar dynasty built a new shrine adjacent to the ruins of the original temple, which had been destroyed by Aurangzeb. This shrine was consecrated in 1785

to rule while also reiterating her female identity via the erection of charitable and religious institutions that reinforce her reputation as "Mata" (mother), and even "Devi" (goddess) Ahilyabai. [131]

Ahilyabai's devotion to jyotirlinga temples demonstrates the intersection of her political aspirations and religious convictions. Her architectural contributions represent just one facet of her extensive religious patronage, which she utilized strategically to establish and reinforce the legitimacy of her governance. The selection and positioning of jyotirlinga and other temples, particularly the specific jyotirlinga temples she reconstructed, served a significant purpose in legitimizing Holkar territory and governance, whilst indicating Holkar authority beyond their established boundaries. The architectural style during Ahilyabai's reign and other Maratha patrons substantially integrated Decani Sultanate elements in both structure and construction material. This represented a distinctive central Indian interpretation of the Mughal-Rajput architectural fusion that had become prevalent across northern and central India by the eighteenth century.

Whilst the Mughal-Rajput architectural style, featuring fluted columns and domes with lotus-petal drums, had become standard for royal constructions in northern India by the 18th century, the temple architecture in central India's Madhya Pradesh and Maharashtra regions displayed a unique evolution and character, applicable to both Hindu and Jain structures. The Maratha-Holkar variant features a predominantly centralized square or octagonal layout, with

131 Cummings Cathleen (2017) "Mapping Holkar: Identity and the Good Name of Ahilyabai." Women, Gender and Art in Asia, c. 1500-1900: 8-33.

entrances adorned with small pavilions, *bangla* cornices[132], and spire-like *shikara* towers[133] with smooth or ribbed surfaces. These Maratha-Holkar structures typically display minimal figurative decorations on their facades and often contain multiple worship areas, including chambers on upper levels and below ground. These edifices possess the architectural magnificence of the northern tradition whilst similarly symbolizing authority and dominance.

Numerous scholars contend, with valid reasoning, that Ahilyabai's main objective appears to have been ensuring devotees had access to worship spaces whilst preventing additional rifts amongst local faith communities. For Ahilyabai, establishing a sacred space for devotional practices held equal significance to constructing an enduring structure that would demonstrate her authority and financial resources. These religious endeavors formed part of Ahilyabai's broader approach to sustain her authority as a ruler. In India, as was common globally, governance was traditionally a male-dominated hereditary privilege. Female rulers, being rare, faced unique challenges. They had to navigate power dynamics within male-centric environments whilst simultaneously earning their subjects' allegiance. These women needed to establish their political authority through more striking visual displays compared to male

---

132 Bangla Cornices refer to a unique architectural feature found in the Bengali style of architecture, particularly in temples and other structures. These cornices are characterized by their curved shape, often used in conjunction with other elements like domes, arches, and vaults. In broader architectural terms, cornices are horizontal decorative moldings that crown a building or furniture element, serving both functional and aesthetic purposes.

133 Shikhara towers are the towering superstructures or spires above the sanctum sanctorum (*garbhagriha*) in North Indian temple architecture, symbolizing a "mountain peak" (Sanskrit: *shikhara*). These towers are a defining feature of the Nagara style of architecture and are often used in Jain temples as well

rulers.[134]

Ahilyabai is one of the towering leaders who stands out as one of the few women in pre-modern South Asia. Her exceptional position as a female leader, coupled with her family's dynastic claims (the Holkars), significantly influenced her extensive architectural projects. In recent decades, feminist art historians have introduced "matronage" as a term to acknowledge women's significant role in historical art commissioning, whilst differentiating their practices from traditional male-dominated artistic patronage. Research into female commissioning has extensively covered the Italian Renaissance, English Georgian and Victorian periods. These analyses explore the contextual factors that influenced prominent women's artistic choices, their selection of artists, and how they utilized these commissions to shape their public personas. Scholars have also investigated the 10th century Chola Queen Sembian Mahadevi's temple commissions in South India, predominantly dedicated to "Siva as Nataraj," the Chola dynasty's patron deity. However, the architectural commissions of Queen Ahilyabai Holkar and their political influence have been overlooked in the growing corpus of scholarship on South Asian matronage because of colonial hegemony and erasure of rich cultural heritage because of the same. That scholars have thus far largely neglected Ahilyabai's architectural matronage as well as her political career, which is surprising as she was one of the most successful female rulers and prolific builders in South

134 Diwan, H. D., Sharma, A., Bhadauria, S. S., Kadwe, P., Sanyal, D., & Sharma, J. (2020). Ancient Hindu rock monuments, configuration and architectural features of Ahilya Devi Fort of Holkar Dynasty, Mahismati Region, Maheshwar, Narmada Valley, Central India. *International Journal of Scientific Development and Research*, *5*(11), 134. Retrieved from https://www.ijsdr.org/

Asian history. Her numerous commissions and architectural renovations span the length of India, as exemplified in the Kedarnath temple at the foothills of Himalaya and the Rameshwaram temple in the southern state of Tamil Nadu, also financed from her personal funds. As illustrated by the examples above, for pre-modern South Asian women to commission works of art and architecture was not without precedent.[135]

However, Ahilyabai's commissions are uncommon in that they were not motivated by a distinct political agenda and were a key facet of her gendered performances of authority, Ahilyabai ascendence to power as a widow when her male relatives were unable to rule the territory was also a relatively new form of establishment. This necessitated the female ruler to develop a distinctive visual representation of her authority in order to establish both dynastic and personal legitimacy. In the absence of female rulership traditions in pre-modern India, women adopted established kingship models from North India's royal predecessors. Ahilyabai combined masculine royal with high-caste Hindu feminine behaviors to reconcile her dual roles of a legitimate ruler and a pious widow. Her commissioning of chhatris (cenotaphs)[136] for Malhar Rao (1693-1766), her father-in-law and Holkar King, exemplified this approach. Chatri's are structures that mark Hindu aristocrats' cremation sites and symbolize their kingship through their names, forms and functions. The act of commissioning chhatris itself conveys political legitimacy, paralleling the eldest son's duty in performing last rites. In northwest India's royal necropolises,

135 Gupta, A. G. (2019). The Women Who Ruled India: Leaders. Warriors. Icons Hachette India

136 Hardy, A. (2007). The temple architecture of India (1st ed.). Wiley

chhatri sequences visually represented succession lines through generations. Ahilyabai's commission of Malhar Rao's notably large chhatris, with their symbolic interior arrangement, reinforced Holkar royal connections and her leadership credentials. Ahilyabai outdid most Indian kings in her public performances of piety, largess, and other aspects of Raja Dharma. [137]

Tumultuous Politics, Raja Dharma, and Performances of Gendered Authority in Early-modern North India

The 18th Century north Indian political landscape was marked by turmoil as several dynasties were trying to fill the void created by the deteriorating Mughal Empire. Among these politically ambitious groups were the Marathas, a Hindu ethnic community comprising several dynasties, including the Holkars, which originated in the Deccan. Initially, the heads of the various Maratha dynasties ruled as subedars (a landed military title) under the Brahmin Peshwas who ruled the Maratha Confederacy, which they founded in the early 18th century, from Pune, Maratha forces quickly expanded their territory northward and subjugated majority of the Hindu Rajput kingdoms in northwest India. Concomitantly, as several Maratha subedars, including Malhar Rao Holkar, advanced further from the Peshwa's orbit of power, they claimed more autonomy, ultimately becoming de facto rulers of the lands, they commanded, rather than vassals to a distant overlord. In 1733, Peshwa Bajirao I granted Malhar Rao the state of Indore, with a capital of the same name.[138]

137 Majumdar, R. C. (1977). The History and Culture of the Indian People: The Maratha Supremacy. Bharatiya Vidya Bhavan

138 Burway, M. W (1925). Life of His Highness Maharaja Tukoji Rao Holkar II, GCSI, Ruler of Indore (1835–1886)

The Rajputs, whom the Marathas subjugated, belong to a subdivision of the elite caste, whose members have historically been the rulers and warriors of north India. The Marathas' conquest of the Rajput kingdoms provided them with both funds and models to establish their own states throughout north and central India. Once ensconced in their new territories, heads of numerous Maratha dynasties quickly evinced their transformation from conquerors and subedars to kings in accordance with Rajput models of kingship. Like other Marathas, Malhar Rao would have been particularly anxious to participate in established expressions of Hindu kingship. Numerous Maratha dynasties were in fact of humble origins. For example, the Holkars were originally hereditary shepherds, a genealogy that hardly recommended them for rulership.[139] To legitimize their new positions of power, Maratha rulers reinvented their lineages and transformed their community into martial kshatriya caste. To this end, Maratha kings employed priests, whose hereditary work was genealogical record keeping, to rewrite their dynastic histories. Among the royal behaviors which Maratha rulers incorporated was the commissioning of philanthropic institutions and chhatris to memorialize their ancestors. Prolific building activity quickly became an outstanding feature of Maratha rule, and no Maratha commissioned more buildings than Ahilyabai.

Maratha royals soon far surpassed their Rajput predecessors in architectural patronage, commissioning forts, temples, Dharamshala (pilgrimage rest houses), *ghatı* (bathing wharves), and *charrís* not only in their own states, but

139 Braddock. M (2017) (Ed.), Women, gender and art in Asia, c. 1500–1900 (p. 41) Memorial, Ahilyabai Holkar's. Royal matronage and a visual vocabulary of Indian queenship. Routledge

throughout India. They also provided on-going support to Brahmin priests at Hindu pilgrimage centers. In their new capitals, the Marathas aggressive architectural patronage was territorial and politically informed, allowing them to visibly lay claim to their new lands. The Marathas would have been especially compelled to impress their presence onto their recently acquired capitals, as these spaces already had protracted histories under the Rajputs and Mughals. In addition to visibly laying claim to their new territories and beyond, Maratha architectural patronage was also a performance of political legitimacy. As established through texts on Hindu statecraft, and the actions of centuries of rulers prior to the 18th century, benevolent gift-giving was an integral component of Indic kingship. For Hindu kings, royal duties are established in the socio-religiously sanctioned concept of *raja dharma*, or duties of a king, which were intended to secure peace and prosperity for their subjects and land. Among these royal duties were patronage of the arts, festivals, and the religious community, and construction and upkeep of philanthropic, educational, and sacred institutions. Ahilyabai outdid most Indian kings in her public performances of piety, largess, and other aspects of rājādharma[140]. One of the largest Maratha commissions is the Holkars' Ahilya Fort, which dominates the skyline of the sacred Hindu city of Maheshwar, Madhya Pradesh. Although Indore was the official Holkar capital, which Ahilyabai transformed from a village backwater into a thriving commercial center, Maheshwar was also an important Holkar center, and Ahilyabai ruled from the Ahilya Fort. In addition to the several other temples throughout the city, Ahilyabai left her

140 Narayan, Jitendra (2004): Relevance of rājādharma of ancient India." The Indian Journal of Political Science 21-28.

mark on the fort with her commission of a monumental Śiva temple, whose śikhara (spire) towers above its curtain wall. The majority of Ahilyabai's sacred commissions throughout India are similarly Śiva temples, as this is the Holkar *iṣṭadevā* (patron deity). In her prolific commissioning and restoration of Śiva temples, Ahilyabai associated herself with this deity and proclaimed him as the source of her power.

Perhaps Ahilyabai's best known sacred commission is her rebuilding of the Kashi Vishvanath Śiva temple in Varanasi in 1777, an act doubtlessly informed as much by politics as by piety. Ahilyabai's active matronage in Varanasi, particularly of this temple, closely associated her with and ingratiate her to the city's powerful Brahmin community, who then supported her rule. One of India's most sacred pilgrimage sites that hundreds of thousands of Hindus still visit annually, the Kashi Vishwanath temple is also a nexus of entangled histories, communal memory, and conflict that unfurled over several centuries.[141]The temple was razed by Muslim rulers and replaced by mosques on several occasions: by Sultan Qutub ud-Din Aibek in 1194, Sultan Sikander Lodi in 1494, and finally, Mughal Emperor Aurangzeb in 1669. After the temple's final demolition, Aurangzeb replaced it with the Alamgir Masjid (popularly known as the Gyan Vapi Mosque), which remains an active site of worship today. Each time prior to Aurangzeb's razing, the temple was rebuilt by prominent Rajputs, such as Raja Todar Mal, finance minister and high-ranking courtier to Mughal Emperor Akbar, in 1585. Although he did not sponsor the temple's rebuilding, amongst Kashi Vishvanath's most illustrious donors is Raja Man Singh Kachhwaha of Amber, who also commissioned

141 Banerjee, A, Kash (2023), The Valiant History of a Sacred Geography New Delhi: Bloomsbury India

several other temples and ghats in the vicinity.[142]

By leaving his impression on this sacred city, Man Singh became intimately associated with its early modern Hindu history, a city which doubtlessly appealed to Ahilyabai and was focus of her public relations program. She also sponsored the construction and rebuilding of numerous ghats along the Ganges, thus appropriating additional patterns of royal commissioning established prior to her rule. Raja Man Singh is widely celebrated as a paradigm of *rājādharma*; he was a prolific builder of forts and temples in his home state as well as at other sites in north India including Varanasi and Vrindavan. He was also closely associated with the Mughal emperors Akbar and Jahangir; in whose armies and courts he served. Man Singh's[143] political and military successes garnered great wealth and prestige for the Kachhwaha. Significantly, Man Singh's enduring public identity is markedly different from that of other Rajput kings, namely the Sisodia's of Mewar,[144] who are remembered for their staunch resistance to the Mughals.

While the Marathas appropriated Rajput models of *rājādharma*, religious and royal traditions and ceremonials, they also fashioned their identities as the Mughals' political heirs. The latter was integral to Maratha imperial designs, they collected taxes from the Rajputs and other

142 Desai, M, (2017). Banaras Reconstructed: Architecture and Sacred Space in a Hindu Holy City (New Delhi: Oxford University Press,

143 Thakur V Vasudeo, Life and Life's work of Shree Devi Ahilya Bai Holkar , Holkar state History, printed by C.M, Shah Modern Printery Limited, Indore available on https://archive.org/details/in.ernet.dli.2015.199825/page/n5/mode/2up?view=theater accessed on September 26,2024.

144 Braddock. M (2017) (Ed.), *Women, gender and art in Asia, c. 1500–1900* (p. 41) Memorial, Ahilyabai Holkar's. Royal matronage and a visual vocabulary of Indian queenship. Routledge

states on behalf of the militarily inept Mughal Emperor, whom they undoubtedly aspired to ultimately replace. Ahilyabai would certainly have considered the pro- Mughal Rajputs Todar Mal and Raja Man Singh apt figures with whom to associate. In rebuilding a prominent temple associated with both figures nearly two centuries later, she announced that she fostered similar political and religious ideologies to these two distinguished Rajputs. Ahilyabai's architectural endeavors in Varanasi established connections with prominent figures of her community. Plaques[145] dedicated to documenting history's reveal that by the late 17th century, Maratha nobility including the Peshwas and distinguished Maharashtrian military and administrative officials, emerged as the primary supporters of religious and non-religious construction throughout the city. Their contributions included sponsorship of temples, ghats and residential structures.[146]

Beyond the city's religious significance, Varanasi held special relevance due to its connection with Shivaji Bhonsle, who established the Maratha state. Various Sanskrit texts praising Shivaji document how after his escape from Aurangzeb's imprisonment, he undertook a pilgrimage to Varanasi, where he offered prayers at significant temples and performed ritual bathing in the Ganga. These accounts challenge the prevalent view of Marathas as disruptive forces who undermined the Mughal Empire, instead portraying them as devout dharmic pilgrims and protectors of the sacred city. These historical accounts additionally highlight Aurangzeb's oppression of Shivaji whilst presenting the latter's success as

145 Ibid

146 Jain, M, (2022) Vishwanath Rises and Rises: The Story of Eternal Kashi New Delhi: Aryan Books International.

a justified (Hindu) victory. Kashi Vishwanath Temple which was reconstructed under Ahilya's patronage which was a humble tribute to her historical roots and her commitment to philanthropy and fundamental aspects of *rājādharma* to an audience of Hindus not only from her own state, but across India.[147]

She also ensured her eternal presence in a city that was associated with the great Shivaji, thereby linking herself to the founder of Maratha political power.[148]

Donating to the Kashi Vishvanath had become such an established performance of north Indian Hindu kingship, which was further ingrained by Ahilyabai's rebuilding, that some six decades later, Ranjit Singh commissioned the gilding of the main śikhara. As Ranjit Singh[149] was the founder of the Sikh Empire, it may be surmised that by 1839, the year of his lavish commission, the site's status as a conveyer of political authority was so potent that it transcended sectarian affiliations.

Strategically building architectural structures without disrupting any harmony

147 Soman, S, Jahagirdar V, Karma Yogini: Life of Ahilyabai Holkar (Mehta Publishing House, 2021), 56-60.

148 Desai, M. (2017). Banaras Reconstructed: Architecture and Sacred Space in a Hindu Holy City. University of Washington Press

149 Ranjit Singh refers to Maharaja Ranjit Singh (1780-1839), the founder and ruler of the Sikh Empire (1799-1839) based in Punjab. He was a powerful and secular-minded ruler who patronized religious and cultural institutions beyond his own Sikh faith. His connection to Kashi Vishwanath Temple is significant because, in 1839, he donated gold to gild the temple's main Śikhara (spire), enhancing its grandeur. This act demonstrated his patronage of Hindu religious sites, reinforcing the temple's status as a symbol of political and spiritual authority that transcended religious boundaries.

Beyond Ahilyabai's decision to rebuild the temple and the messages of political authority that communicated, the choice of location too was strategic.

Ahilyabai demonstrated remarkable cultural sensitivity by constructing the current Vishvanath temple beside the Alamgiri Masjid, instead of demolishing Aurangzeb's Mosque, which could have triggered religious tensions. Her approach reflected a thoughtful consideration of the diverse religious character of this significant Hindu pilgrimage destination. For Ahilyabai and her contemporaries in the 18th century, the rebuilding of Kashi Vishwanath likely served as another element in establishing her authority. These patronages for reconstructing Hindu temples paved the way for spiritual nationalism instilling in the people of Bharat the spirit of oneness. She created a network of roads connecting all major Hindu sites which allowed people to move fearlessly across the nation. Her architectural marvels were not only driven by religious purpose but was to elevate the sense of oneness and togetherness in the people of Bharat.

The British, notably, held her in high regard. Sir John Malcolm documented in the 1820s: "Ahilyabai's extraordinary ability won her the regard of her subjects and of the other Maratha confederates. With the natives of Malwa... her name is sainted and she (is viewed as) Incarnation of the Divinity. In the soberest view that can be taken of her character, she certainly appears... to have been one of the purest and most exemplary rulers that ever existed."[150] Though she preceded the British Raj,

150 Jahagirdar, V. (1991). Karma Yogini (Ahilyabai Holkar) (9th ed.). Mehta Publishing House. ISBN: 9788177664553.

her legacy influenced independence movement leaders. Jawaharlal Nehru cited her reign as proof of Indian self-governance capabilities: "Ahilya's reign has become almost legendary as a period during which perfect order and good government prevailed, and the people prospered. She was a very able ruler and organizer, highly respected during her lifetime, and considered as a saint by grateful people after her death." Similarly, British-born INC president, Annie Besant, idolized Ahilya's reign as one in which Indians of all ethnicities and religions lived harmoniously. Many sources attest to her demonstrating care for her subjects, she is still celebrated as a ruler who left her land in a considerably better position than she inherited it.

Agricultural Practices, Water management and building of Embankments at Narmada

Ahilyabai showed foresight in environmental conservation through her governance and her infrastructure projects. She understood ecological sustainability and their effects on subsequent generations. In today's world. climate change poses significant challenges, and her principles offer valuable insights for contemporary administrators in developing sustainable policies that ensure both societal progress and environmental conservation. She enhanced the Narmada River basin through effective agricultural practices, water management systems, and embankment construction. Throughout her reign (1767-1795),[151] her practical approach to resource management established enduring prosperity in an area previously susceptible to floods and droughts.

151 Jahagirdar, V. (1991). *Karma Yogini (Ahilyabai Holkar)* (9th ed.). Mehta Publishing House. ISBN: 9788177664553.

Ahilyabai implemented agricultural policies based on her comprehensive knowledge of regional conditions. She understood that the Narmada's irregular flow patterns necessitated organized intervention for stable crop production. Her administration introduced crop rotation to preserve soil quality, whilst diverse crop cultivation reduced risks associated with weather variations and market changes. She notably encouraged the production of cash crops such as cotton alongside food crops, creating a stable agricultural economy. She supported the use of superior seed varieties, acquired through trading relationships with adjacent regions. The resulting agricultural abundance enabled the kingdom to sustain itself during scarce periods and conduct profitable commerce. Ahilyabai's significant achievement was her extensive water management programmes along the Narmada. Understanding water availability as the key factor in agricultural success, she established comprehensive water conservation and distribution systems:[152]

- She directed the building of numerous tanks and *talabs* (reservoirs) to store monsoon rainfall for dry periods.
- Her government restored *vavs* (old step wells) and built additional ones to access underground water during droughts.
- A canal system linked these water sources to farmlands, ensuring efficient water distribution.
- Small check dams on tributary streams reduced water velocity, limiting erosion, and improving ground water levels.

152 Desai, M. (2017). *Banaras Reconstructed: Architecture and Sacred Space in a Hindu Holy City*. University of Washington Press

These implementations changed farming methods regionally, allowing continuous cultivation in previously seasonal farming areas. Historical sources indicate that her governed villages rarely faced water shortages, even when surrounding areas experienced drought. Her flood management strategy demonstrated exceptional planning.[153] She recognized the potential advantages of controlled annual floods. Her embankment projects reflected this understanding. The main embankments were constructed to direct river flow rather than completely restrict it, protecting communities and valuable farmland whilst permitting controlled flooding in designated areas. This regulated flooding deposited fertile silt that enriched fields naturally. Her engineering teams incorporated ghats into embankment designs, providing water access for farming and household use. These structures utilized local materials, primarily stone and compressed earth, enabling local communities to maintain them effectively. Historical accounts show Ahilyabai inspected these projects personally, often allocating resources to reinforce vulnerable areas before monsoons. This direct involvement ensured practical solutions to actual challenges. The systems Ahilyabai established remained functional well beyond her reign. Many water management structures she commissioned continued to operate up till recent times, some serving communities after 200 years. Her comprehensive river management approach, combining flood protection with water conservation and agricultural requirements, established a framework that influenced subsequent regional development. Contemporary specialists studying

153 Vaidya S (2024) Swarajya Magazine, "That Evening By The Narmada, Where Devi Ahilyabai Might Have Once Stood" accessed retrieved from https://swarajyamag.com/culture/that-evening-by-the-narmada-where-devi-ahilyabai-might-have-once-stood accessed on December 22nd 2024.

traditional water management note that her innovations align with current sustainable development principles. The economic success generated by these agricultural and water management improvements allowed Ahilyabai to support her renowned public works and continue to do charity work throughout India.

Ahilya Devi Holkar introduced several progressive reforms to encourage farmers and promote self-reliance. She was a visionary as she was one of the first to lead people into animal husbandry as a complementary activity to farming, increasing both income and agricultural productivity. She adopted mixed cropping and the cultivation of spices as cash crops, especially on the fertile banks of the Narmada River. Her promotion of orchards and fruit cultivation diversified farming and improved the common people's diet. Understanding the value of forest produce, Ahilya Devi expanded markets for fruits and honey, providing new livelihood opportunities for Adivasis. This initiative further led to significant forest conservation in which forest yields were obtained; hence, the green cover in her state increased. The Holkar state generated substantial revenue, including tributes and regional taxes. One notable system was the Bhilkawadi tax, which gave Bhil communities the right to collect tolls in their regions. These reduced incidents of robbery, making routes safer for traders and pilgrims and integrating the Bhils into administration. She undertook comprehensive agricultural reforms, distributing quality seeds, tools, and cattle, encouraging group farming, and promoting experimentation at government farms. Experts at Maheshwar tested seeds and studied soil fertility, weather patterns, and disease control, helping farmers adopt more scientific methods.

A visionary in water management, Ahilya Devi constructed bunds, tanks, wells, and canals across regions like Jejuri, Maheshwar, Ambad, and Trimbakeshwar, utilizing her private funds. These structures effectively harvested rainwater, and many of them still supply water today. Through her innovative and inclusive policies, Ahilya Devi not only improved agricultural output but also ensured sustainable rural development and public welfare.

CHAPTER - 5

Entrepreneurial Leadership and Economic Empowerment in Ahilyabai Holkar's Legacy

Rani Ahilyabai Holkar's rule incorporated comprehensive economic growth and cultural conservation alongside traditional governance. Her leadership established Maheshwar as a prominent textile production hub, specifically in the Maheshwari handloom industry. She created weaving facilities that generated employment opportunities, particularly for women and families. Her administration supported artisans with resources, training, and patronage to improve their skills. She implemented balanced trade practices, developed markets, and established quality standards. The distinctive Maheshwari weaving patterns she introduced featured regional designs and architectural elements. Her business-focused strategy created lasting employment whilst safeguarding traditional practices. The state experienced substantial financial growth under her governance with the yearly revenue, which was Rs. 75 lakhs during the reign of her father-in-law Malhar Rao Holkar, increased to Rs. one crore five lakhs during her rule.[154] The financial management, backing of local industries and well-structured taxation system, contributed to economic growth significantly. Her leadership was different from other rulers of the time due to her strategic allocation of government resources. Further, public welfare programme, infrastructure development and trade expansion contributed to sustained economic growth and prosperity.

Maheshwari Sarees: A Cultural Enterprise for Economic and Social Empowerment

The nine-yard fabric known as saree has transformed into an intrinsic part of Indian clothing. This traditional attire symbolizing dignity, perfection, and uniqueness of women, whilst maintaining the cultural legacy of India's handloom craftsmanship is what stood out. Situated in Khargone district of Madhya Pradesh, handloom weaving represented feminine grace, elegance, and cultural heritage to the populace then and continues to be that way for the populace to this day. Their unique motifs and rich heritage make them emblematic of India's traditional weaving mastery and cultural legacy. The artisans originally specialized in crafting turbans for royal families before transitioning to silk saree weaving. Their intricate border patterns draw inspiration from the architectural grandeur of royal forts, stately gateways, ornate ceiling designs, and the flowing Narmada River. Under her governance, the administration became a primary purchaser of these handcrafted sarees.

154 Thakur V Vasudeo, Life and Life's work of Shree Devi Ahilya Bai Holkar , Holkar state History, printed by C.M, Shah Modern Printery Limited, Indore available on https://archive.org/details/in.ernet.dli.2015.199825/page/n5/mode/2up?view=theater accessed on September 26,2024.

During her queenship, the state acquired volumes of woven sarees, and their recognition steadily spread throughout the country, and presently they have garnered worldwide appeal. Different grades of silk from Bangalore, along with China silk, cotton materials, Kosa, various forms of Jari, and Khadi fabric are utilized in the production. These handloom sarees remain unique and captivating, with craftspeople creating each piece through their personal innovation and artistic expression. The manufacturing process started with Bana, the first step in which unprocessed silk is organized and spooled onto a reel. After that, the silk is moved to a metal rod, referred to as Tana and then they attach this prepared silk to the loom through a technique called Jodi. Before starting the process, they needed to visualize and develop a blueprint of the design pattern. After setting up the design pattern on the loom, weaver started making a new saree with a distinct design. The weaving process of the sarees that approximately took a week to be completed included different silk types sourced from Bangalore, combined with China silk, cotton materials, Kosa, different varieties of Jari and Khadi fabrics.

History of Maheshwari Handloom Sarees

The Queen wished to design a saree that would merge elegance with ease of wear, making sure it remained light and manageable. According to historical records, she made sure that talented craftsmen from Surat and Malwa regions came to make sarees, which she presented as gifts to visiting royalty and her own family members.[155] The distinctive attire

155 Maheshwari, N. (2024). *Rashtra Sevika Maa Ahilyabai Holkar: Queen of Malwa Indian History & Cultural Stories Book in Hindi*. Prabhat Prakashan Pvt Ltd. ISBN: 9789355623753.

later gained recognition as Maheshwari sarees. Historical documents indicate that Queen Ahilyabai herself created the first design pattern. Whilst originally reserved for aristocratic ladies, these traditional garments are presently available in both local and international markets.[156] She demonstrated an appreciation for design aesthetics and her creative vision was shaped by the intricate patterns and detailed carvings adorning the Maheshwar fort and temple structure and the design originate from the architectural features present on the walls of Maheshwar Fort. The patterns in these sarees include the *Chatai* (Mat) design, *Chameli ka Phool* (Chameli flower) arrangement, *Eent* (Brick) configuration and *Heera* (Diamond) layout.[157] Initially crafted from pure silk, these sarees evolved to include pure cotton and silk-cotton blends, and now they have introduced wool also into the production technique. These sarees which were in comparison light in weight, made for a different alternative option compared to the heavier Kanchipuram sarees of South India. The early Maheshwari sarees featured deep hues including red, maroon, black, purple and green but the newer versions we see today now include lighter shades and incorporate gold and silver threads. The traditional color palette, known in local terminology, includes *Angoori* (grape green), *Dalimbi* (deep pink), *Gul Bakshi* (magenta), *Jaamla* (purple), *Tapkeer* (deep brown), *Aamrak* (golden), *Rani* (deep pink), *Dhaani* (green) and *Kaashi* (light purple). The dyeing process typically utilizes vegetable-based colorants. These sarees typically feature either a plain body or incorporate various patterns of stripes and checks. *Chandrakala* and *Baingani Chandrakala* represent plain variants, whilst *Chandratara*

156 Dongerkery, K. S. (1959). The Indian Sari. Bombay: The Popular Book Depot

157 Singh, M. (2023). Saris of Memory. Roli Books

Beli and *Parbi* showcase striped and checked patterns.[158]

Another beautiful characteristic of these sarees is their reversible border, locally referred to as *Bugdi* The production involves sourcing materials from various locations: cotton is obtained from Coimbatore in South India, silk comes from Bangalore, whilst wool is imported from Australia. The final stages of production take place in Kolkata, where the material undergoes processing before women weavers in Maheshwar complete the textile. The price range for an authentic piece varies from Rs. one thousand five hundred to Rs. 20 thousand. Due to Maheshwar's prominence as a central Indian kingdom and its ties to Shivaji's Maratha empire, royal visitors frequently came to Maa Ahilya Bai's capital. During one such visit, Rajmata conceived a plan to present the royal guests with gifts that would showcase Maheshwar's heritage. She implemented her innovative idea by inviting skilled weavers from Surat and Mandu to produce the inaugural collection of Maheshwari handloom sarees. These featured distinctive designs incorporating local architectural and artistic elements, with detailed patterns on the borders and striking pallu designs. These creations were named Garbh Reshmi sarees, and the production involved a technique that combined silk and cotton to create an airy fabric. *Garbh Reshmi* denotes silk from the womb, referring to premium silk obtained from specific silkworm cocoons. Their borders displayed geometric patterns, whilst the pallu featured detailed illustrations, often including peacocks, elephants, and various fauna. The sarees utilized vivid colors, particularly favoring red, green and gold shades. Eventually,

158 Maheshwari, N. (2024). Rashtra Sevika Maa Ahilyabai Holkar: Queen of Malwa Indian History & Cultural Stories Book in Hindi. Prabhat Prakashan Pvt Ltd. ISBN: 9789355623753.

the traditional *Garbh Reshmi* weaving technique declined, giving way to pure silk and cotton fabric usage. Nevertheless, these sarees' influence persisted, with their intricate patterns and motifs continuing to shape contemporary Maheshwari saree designs. These elegant garments served as distinguished presents for esteemed guests, symbolizing warmth, and reverence. As fashion sensibilities progressed, Maheshwari sarees also changed. The original cotton fabric gave way to silk, whilst the patterns became more sophisticated and detailed. Now these sarees are celebrated for seamlessly combining classical and modern design aesthetics. Be it in terms of promoting cultural activities and Maheshwari sarees or generating employment opportunities for numerous individuals. The town of Maheshwar attracted thousands of sculptors, artisans and statuaries seeking work opportunities and under her leadership, it emerged as a textile manufacturing hub in the country. She actively recruited skilled weavers from across the nation, helping them establish themselves and seek employment. She financially supported entrepreneurs and by backing their products and acquiring their merchandise, particularly sarees and textile products. Due to royal support, the craftsmen were inspired to create superior quality fabrics featuring detailed artistic patterns in Maheshwar. Devi Ahilya herself consistently donned Maheshwar-crafted sarees. The weaving industry prospered due to her substantial patronage and sophisticated preferences, resulting in enhanced prosperity for the craftsmen community. Her patronage of arts, literature, and architecture considerably enriched central India's cultural legacy, notably shaping the artistic traditions of the Malwa region. She ensured that business initiatives and innovative ventures were encouraged. She took to improving infrastructure and commercial networks during her governance which laid the foundation for economic advancement.

Cultural Entrepreneurship: The Enduring Legacy of Maheshwari Sarees

Maheshwar became synonymous with the handloom industry and provided a livelihood to artisans all while enabling local economic activity. These sarees gained their distinctive appearance from the detailed architectural features of Maheshwar Fort, featuring characteristic patterns like *Chatai* (Mat), *Chameli ka Phool* (Chameli Flower), *Eent* (Brick), and *Heera* (Diamond). While it is true that she gave extensive financial support to craftspeople, she also secured essential raw materials and actively marketed these fabrics throughout India. This yielded substantial socio-economic outcomes. The women gained financial autonomy and contributed to their family's earnings. Their social position improved considerably, breaking away from conventional domestic responsibilities. The employment framework she established continues to provide livelihood opportunities for numerous women in the region in present times. Organizations now have also adopted similar inclusive economic approaches. The Self-Employed Women's Association (SEWA) now facilitates skill development and market opportunities for women artisans. Fab India and Dastkar also support traditional weavers by connecting them to domestic and international markets.

Infrastructure Development and Trade Expansion

She built networks of roads, bazaars and warehouses to strengthen trade activities. She implemented business-friendly policies with balanced taxation and removed trade barriers to encourage commercial growth. These progressive measures transformed Maheshwar into a prominent textile manufacturing center, drawing numerous craftspeople, artists and merchants looking for prosperity. The arrival of skilled workers established Maheshwar as a thriving commercial center, leading to self-sufficiency and sustained financial growth.

Comparing Cultural Entrepreneurship Globally

The economic empowerment strategies of Ahilyabai share commonalities with notable international figures in cultural enterprise. Similar to her work, "Coco Chanel" transformed French fashion whilst promoting women's economic engagement through textile and design sectors. In the 16th century, Queen Elizabeth I supported England's wool trade, which became vital to the nation's economic success. The patronage of Maheshwari sarees by Ahilyabai demonstrates how cultural industries serve as drivers of economic growth. The economic approaches of Rani Ahilyabai Holkar uniquely combined cultural conservation with commercial innovation. Her support of Maheshwari sarees preserved cultural heritage whilst creating a robust industry that employed numerous artisans. Her progressive policies on trade, taxation and women's participation fostered an economy that benefited all sections of society. Her governance style, which united cultural enterprise with economic planning, remains a valuable reference for today's leaders. The success of her initiatives is evident in Maheshwar's present-day handloom sector. The core principles she established, including fair economic participation, support for artisans, and balanced trade policies, maintain their significance in contemporary times, showcasing the lasting impact of her administrative wisdom.

Understanding Cultural and Creative Industries as Development Catalysts

In Maheshwar during the 18th century, Ahilya Bai Holkar established an integrated system balancing artistic merit, economic sustainability and social progress. Contemporary successful social-cultural enterprises in traditional craft revival often adopt the comprehensive approach demonstrated in historical patronage systems. These strategies recognize that cultural preservation, economic sustainability, and community advancement require simultaneous attention rather than isolated or sequential treatment. Whilst DiMaggio (1982),[159] Ellmeier (2003),[160] and Lounsbury & Glynn (2001) [161] advocate distinguishing traditional entrepreneurship from cultural variants, debates persist regarding the discrete nature of social entrepreneurship. Our examination positions social entrepreneurship within the context of cultural heritage and cultural capital. We suggest a unified social-cultural entrepreneurship domain that serves a distinct function in contemporary economics, rather than treating these as separate entities. DiMaggio's analysis focused on "culture capitalists" who recognized cultural opportunities

159 Maggio P(1982), "Cultural Entrepreneurship in Nineteenth-Century Boston: The Creation of an Organizational Base for High Culture in America," Media, Culture & Society 4, no. 1: 33–50.

160 Ellmeier A (2003), "Cultural Entrepreneurialism: On the Changing Relationship Between the Arts, Culture and Employment," International Journal of Cultural Policy 9, no. 1: 3–16.

161 Lounsbury M and Glynn M.A (2001), "Cultural Entrepreneurship: Stories, Legitimacy, and the Acquisition of Resources," Strategic Management Journal 22, no. 6–7 : 545–564.

and accepted associated risks to create culturally significant products. In this context, culture determines both operational boundaries and societal cultural interpretation. Traditional perspectives regard art and culture as exclusive sectors where commercial activities potentially diminish authenticity. This study questions the necessity of protecting art forms from commercialization. Instead, it positions social-cultural entrepreneurship within profitable frameworks, viewing it as the commercial development of traditional arts, with the aim of generating income to sustain these practices within their original communities. The resultant social value addresses issues of unemployment and enhances social metrics, thereby encouraging artisans to maintain their cultural legacy. UNESCO[162] defines Cultural and Creative Industries (CCIs) as "activities whose principal purpose is production or reproduction, promotion, distribution or commercialization of goods, services, and activities of a cultural, artistic, or heritage-related nature." These encompass arts and crafts, gastronomy, tourism, museums, design, fashion, performing arts, visual arts, festivals, literature, printing, advertising, and occasionally traditional medicine and arts-based therapies. Market valuation of traditional arts through cultural economy commercialization drives economic growth. These cultural products enable international trade whilst providing substantial income for artisan communities. Microfinance and creation of self-help groups are two important components for developing skill-based entrepreneurship. Modern financial inclusion

162 UNESCO (United Nations Educational, Scientific and Cultural Organization) is a specialized agency of the United Nations that promotes international collaboration in education, science, culture, and communication. Established on 16 November 1945, UNESCO aims to foster peace and security by encouraging dialogue among civilizations and sustainable development through cultural preservation, scientific cooperation, and educational advancement

tools provide credit access to marginalized groups, fostering independence and social development. Similarly, Ahilyabai Holkar also supported artisans through state-backed economic programmes and utilized royal patronage for community development. Microfinance outcomes vary according to implementation philosophy, population needs alignment and staff dedication. Naila Kabeer[163] identifies microfinance organizations' role in addressing institutional exclusion of poor individuals from formal banking. Indian microfinance setups that turned out to be a primary poverty alleviation tool, engaged women through collective approaches including the Grameen model, self-help groups and cooperatives, offering social transformation potential. They gave credit access to those excluded from traditional banking. These institutions, supported by donors, NGOs or commercial banks, provide small loans to disadvantaged entrepreneurs and individuals.

Traditional arts rejuvenation via social enterprises benefits women's progresses significantly, as exemplified by Ahilya Bai's pioneering administration that bolstered craft communities. Research confirms that participation in cultural programmes and community groups can elevate women's societal position. This transformational approach of Ahilya Bai's governance, which elevated entire communities through sustainable practices. The combination of social and cultural entrepreneurship offers an effective structure for preserving traditional arts whilst addressing artisan community challenges. By combining cultural product viability with social welfare aims, these initiatives can maintain cultural heritage whilst improving living conditions.

163 Kabeer, N (2005), Inclusive Citizenship: Meanings and Expressions, London: Zed Books

The Revival of Traditional Handloom in Maheshwar: A Case Study of the Rehwa Society's Intervention[164]

Her support for Maheshwari weaver has laid the foundation for the Rehwa Society, a nonprofit organization working for weaver the vision of the society aligns with idea of holistic empowerment of the folk artist and revival of Folk arts. The Revival of Traditional Handloom in Maheshwar: A Case Study of the Rehwa Society's Intervention. Revival of handloom weaving in Maheshwar analyses how the Rehwa Society, established by the royal couple Richard Shivaji Rao and Sally Holkar, successfully revitalized the dying Maheshwari weaving tradition through different adaptations in production processes, weaver welfare, and market engagement.[165] A heritage craft form evolved from near extinction to a thriving economic activity, showing how the viability of traditional crafts exists in contemporary markets when supported by institutional frameworks and market strategies. Maheshwar which was once known for its craftsmanship and weaving style because of Queen Ahilya Bai Holkar in the 19th century also started declining to a great extent in the mid 1970s to the point where it would almost be extinct, with only approximately 50 functional looms remaining. The Rehwa Society's interventions transformed this declining trade into a commercial enterprise again. A blend of tradition and innovation, welfare and commerce, and local production and global market force in craft led to this revival.

The Rehwa Society's approach to revival was characterized by

164 Mathur N (2006), Rehwa: Maheshwari Handloom Weavers, EPW Vol. 41, Issue No. 31.

165 Mathur N (2006), Rehwa: Maheshwari Handloom Weavers, EPW Vol. 41, Issue No. 31.

an organic, iterative methodology that responded to emerging challenges rather than implementing a predetermined blueprint. This approach allowed for various changes across the value chain, implemented depending on resource constraints and immediate needs. Basically, an "emergent strategy" that allows for adaptation while maintaining focus on core objectives. The society's first significant intervention addressed the disorganized production system and low weaver morale. Rehwa established in-house looms where weavers worked on a piece-rate basis instead of working independently. This manufacturing model, similar to the traditional master weaver system, transferred risk from individual weavers to the organization, which proved to be critical for craftspeople to return to their traditional livelihood while feeling safe.

Rates were based on design complexity to ensure weavers received fair compensation for intricate work. Performance incentives were introduced to encourage quality craftsmanship and timely completion of tasks. A rigorous quality control protocol was enforced, involving multiple levels of supervision to maintain high standards. Additionally, strategic inventory and working capital management allowed for efficient resource utilization. To address the challenge of skilled dyeing, local expertise was developed through an incubation programme. Educational facilities for weavers' children were also introduced. Accessible medical services were provided to support the health and well-being of the community. Housing projects on leased govt land offered stable living conditions, and homeowners were given additional looms to increase their earning potential. Furthermore, formal benefits such as provident funds were implemented, providing financial security and reinforcing long-term sustainability for the weavers. The housing project exemplifies the society's integration of welfare and production objectives. By providing housing with additional looms, Rehwa simultaneously addressed social needs while increasing production capacity and household income.

The target segment section focused exclusively on high-end consumers who valued exclusivity and were willing to pay premium prices. Product innovation at Rehwa ensured that while traditional techniques were preserved, the product line continuously evolved to meet market demands. Other than just traditional sarees, they started to include dress materials, shawls, dupattas, stoles, and scarves, which increased its appeal. Experimentation with new materials such as various silks, wool, and zari, and different yarn counts, and weave structures were developed. Collaborations with other craft clusters, such as Bagh block-printing, also added value. To further please consumers, Rehwa introduced theme-based collections for exhibition. Rehwa avoided traditional wholesale and retail channels due to margin constraints and instead adopted a more strategic sales approach. The society employed full-time designers based in major market centers (Delhi and Mumbai) who conducted market assessments, created saleable designs, and guided production planning. This specialized marketing function ensured market relevance while maintaining quality standards.

Starting with just 12 women operating six looms in 1978, Rehwa's organization grew to accommodate 120 operational looms with an equal number of weavers, alongside 75 staff members overseeing production and welfare initiatives. The society's yearly output reached 50,000 meters, ensuring a turnover of Rs. 1.3-1.4 crore. The area now encompasses 1,500 looms and 3,000 weavers, generating a combined yearly turnover of Rs. 6 crores. So, an entire network of businesses, including master craftsmen, yarn providers, dyers, transport services and financial institutions, was in place that led to its sustainability. This multiplication effect illustrates how focused initiatives can stimulate comprehensive economic and cultural renewal. The Rehwa example provides valuable insights into craft revival and development strategies. The organization effectively balanced tradition preservation with progressive innovation, implementing "anchored innovation" - retaining traditional methods whilst adapting designs and materials for contemporary markets. Rehwa's strategy mirrors Ahilya Bai Holkar's historical craft patronage philosophy. The organization's comprehensive involvement across the value chain demonstrates the necessity of systematic intervention in craft revival

CHAPTER - 6

Ahilyabai: An Epitome of Nari Shakti in Contemporary Context

Ahilya Bai proved herself to be a leader who set an example for the women of her era by defying orthodoxy. To put things into context, in the 1700s when certain practices were deeply entrenched in society such as the practice of purdah (seclusion and veiling of women), she challenged these practices by her way of living, governance and leadership. She redefined traditional gender roles and she serves as a testament that women have the potential to be great leaders and engage and contribute to the making of the nation. After the untimely death of her husband, Khanderao Holkar, and the passing of her father-in-law, Malhar Rao Holkar, she emerged as the "De Facto Ruler" of the Malwa kingdom. Through various accounts of a myriad of historians, feminist authors and more, it becomes clear that she earned the absolute obedience and respect of her subjects, from the noble Tukoji Rao Holkar to the commonest village despite living in a society where women were largely confined to domestic roles. Her governance was defined by her assuming herself to be as a true trustee of the state, treating her role as a responsibility to her people rather than a position of privilege.

A Tale of Courage and Vision

With her head covered in Pallu which represents a symbol of elegance, humility, and spiritual devotion, she defied orthodox societal expectations of roles being assigned to women which confined them within the four walls of the house, during this time she dared to step out and increased her visibility in public spaces and her involvement and engagement in administration. Draping the pallu over one's head signified reverence towards seniors, customs, and divine beings, rather than subordination.[166] In the Foucauldian sense she was truly powerful.[167] Her governance model was not operating on a simple top-down authority but a continuous flow through social institutions, relationships, and practices, creating a strong social and cultural capital. Power serves not only as a restrictive force but also as a generative one, creating individuals, regulating bodies, and establishing standards.

Devi Ahilya redefined and reimagined the roles of women in the society. She proved that women were not mere ornaments or secondary citizens, but visionary leaders, astute decision-makers, and game-changers. By stepping out of the zenana and claiming her rightful place in the halls of power, she showed the power of feminine potential, inspiring generations to come. She held regular public meetings, and spoke to the citizens, especially women, which set a precedent for transparent and people-centric governance and earned her the love and respect of her people. What is also noteworthy is what she achieved in a society where women

166 Ball, Stephen J (2012.) Foucault, Power, and Education. Routledge,

167 Foucault, M (1980). Power/Knowledge: Selected Interviews and Other Writings 1972–1977 – A collection of interviews and essays where Foucault elaborates on how power is decentralized and operates through social relations.

were largely excluded from public decision-making. Her meetings were a beacon of hope, inclusivity, providing a platform for common folk to voice their concerns. As most rulers maintained a distance from their subjects, this level of interaction and that too, for a woman in a leadership role was awe-inspiring.

She emerged as an epitome of women empowerment and inclusive governance, her rule was now being seen as an example of how women could excel in roles traditionally dominated by men such as administration, military strategy, and public welfare. Her tenure as a queen created a counter-narrative to the existing view of women being as passive and powerless but created a new narrative wherein women could be active participants in shaping their communities and nations. Her life remains a testament to the transformative power of shattering the shackles and redefining societal expectations. Her exemplary leadership serves as a strong reminder of the potential for women to transcend societal constraints and achieve greatness.

"She was praised by the Britishers as well for her rule and administration,"[168] writes Malcolm, in his writings about the Maratha period.[169] He spoke highly of her administration and emphasized her unique leadership style, which combined administrative excellence with deep spiritual and cultural sensibilities. Malcolm particularly praised her for maintaining a stable and prosperous kingdom during a turbulent period in Indian history. Sir John Malcolm writes about her, forty years after her death, "Her first principle of Government

168 Cummings, C. (2017): Mapping Holkar: Identity and the Good Name of Ahilyabai. Women, Gender and Art in Asia, c. 1500-1900 8-33.

169 Malcolm J (1823), *Memoir of Central India*, vol. 1,London: Kingsbury, Parbury, and Allen, 160–162.

appears to have been moderate assessment and an almost sacred respect for the native rights of the village officers and proprietary land. She heard every complaint in person and although she continually referred cases to the courts of equity and arbitration ... She was always accessible, patient and unwearied in the investigation of most insignificant cases when appeals were made to her for decision."

She was a legend in Malcolm's time (the 1830s and 1840s), as she remains today, for the help she gave widows in keeping their husband's wealth, rather than surrendering it to the state or greedy relatives or managers. The British East India Company, which often interacted with Indian rulers, also recognized Ahilya Bai's governance. British officers such as John Malcolm, in his book *A Memoir of Central India*, praised her for maintaining peace and prosperity in her kingdom during tumultuous times. Malcolm noted her administrative acumen and described her as "one of the purest and most exemplary rulers of her time." He further commented on her ability to command respect from both her subjects and her adversaries, a rare feat for a woman ruler in 18th-century India.

Status and Condition of Women in the Holkar State (1734-1948)[170]

The Holkar State was established in 1734 A.D. and stood out among the Maratha states of Malwa and Central India, such as Gwalior and Dhar, for the relatively better social and political status of its women. This text examines the status and general condition of women in the Holkar State from

170 Sharma K (1978) "Status and Condition of Women in the Holkar State (1734-1948)," *Proceedings of the Indian History Congress* 39, no. II: 801-807.

its inception to 1948. In the mid-18th century, the condition of women in the Maratha states, as in the rest of India, was far from satisfactory. Within the ruling elite and among the Brahmins and Marathas of the Holkar State, women held a relatively better position. Though their numbers were small, women in these privileged classes often wielded influence, especially when married to men of rank. Some can directly be a part of state affairs, and own independent estates assigned to them by their husbands[171].

Several women in the Holkar State were given positions of power because of their intelligence and political acumen, wielding significant influence in the court. Other women from the ruling elite distinguished themselves in warfare and governance. Bhimabai, Malhar Rao Holkar's twenty-year-old widowed sister, led her cavalry against the British at the Battle of Mehdipur in 1817. Kesari Bai, Malhar Rao's mother, administered the state until 1829. After Malhar Rao's death, Gautamabai and Kesari Bai played a decisive role in securing Martand Rao's succession in 1834, just as Ma Sahiba Krishnabai facilitated the accession of Tukoji Rao II in 1844. During his reign, Krishnabai, with the Council of Regency, managed state affairs effectively. In Hindu tradition, wives were regarded as co-sharers of their husbands' prosperity. Malhar Rao Holkar institutionalized this belief by establishing a separate welfare department, Khasgi, in honor of his wife, Gautamabai. The Khasgi jagirs functioned as a self-governing system, independent of the state administration, with separate seals, a Dewan, judicial regulations, and governance. Orders issued by the ruler were

171 Nagrale, N. N (1979). Ahilyabai and her benevolent administration, Proceedings of the Indian History Congress Vol.40.pp 700-706. Indian History Congress retrived on www.jstor.org/stable/44142013

distinct from those issued by the Maharani in the Khasgi territories.

After Gautam Bai's death in 1761, these rights were conferred upon Ahilyabai, and the tradition continued until the Holkar State's dissolution. Income from these estates funded charitable causes, temple construction, and the maintenance of religious sites across India. While rulers hesitated from interfering in Khasgi administration, cases of mismanagement occasionally arose. In 1883, due to mounting complaints from the public, Tukoji Rao II briefly placed Khasgi lands under direct state supervision. During the middle of the nineteenth century, women's education advanced in the Holkar State.[172] The first schools for girls were established in Indore in 1867 during Tukoji Rao Holkar II's reign, with connections to the Indore Madrassa. The academic year 1885-86 saw an increase to three girls' schools, accommodating 94 pupils. The expansion of formal education mostly helped middle-class women, while aristocratic women continued with their private tutors. Due to the decline in purdah practices, women engaged in the public sphere more. The visit of Swami Dayanand Saraswati to Indore in 1881 led to the rise of the Arya Samaj[173] becoming a powerful agent of social change. The organization took a strong stance against child marriage, purdah, and prevalent superstitions, whilst advocating for women's education and supporting the right of widows to remarry. The Holkar Durbar enacted progressive laws, including the Indore

172 Thakur V Vasudeo, Life and Life's work of Shree Devi Ahilya Bai Holkar , Holkar state History, printed by C.M, Shah Modern Printery Limited, Indore available on https://archive.org/details/in.ernet.dli.2015.199825/page/n5/mode/2up?view=theater accessed on September 26,2024.

173 Arya Samaj is a Hindu reform movement founded by Swami Dayanand Saraswati in 1875 in Bombay (now Mumbai).

Hindu Widow Remarriage Act (1915)[174], which legalized widow remarriage, barring cases involving girls under sixteen. The Indore Civil Marriage Act [175] provided legal recognition for inter-caste marriages. The Prohibition of Marriage Between Old Men and Minor Girls Act (1927)[176] set age restrictions for grooms at fifty years. The Indore Divorce Act (1928)[177] granted equal divorce rights to both genders. In 1925, primary education was made mandatory for girls aged six to eleven. Prostitution was outlawed in 1929, and women's property rights were recognized in 1940. Dowry was criminalized in 1941, while maternity benefits were introduced in 1936 and expanded in 1941. By the 1930s, women had become more aware of their rights and joined the national independence movement. By the time of India's freedom struggle, women of the Holkar State became actively involved in the struggle for freedom. By the 1930s, at time of India's freedom struggle, women of the Holkar State had transitioned from passive observers to active participants in shaping their destinies. They had actively rejected regressive practices.

174 To protect what it considered family honor and family property, Hindu society had long disallowed the remarriage of widows, even child and adolescent ones, all of whom were expected to live a life of austerity and abnegation. The Hindu Widows' Remarriage Act provided legal safeguards against loss of certain forms of inheritance for remarrying a Hindu widow, though, under the Act, the widow forsook any inheritance due her from her deceased husband.

175 The Special Marriage Act, 1954 is an act of the Parliament of India with provision for secular civil marriage (or registered marriage) for people of India and all Indian nationals in foreign countries, irrelevant of the religion or faith followed (both for inter-religious couples and also for atheists and agnostics) by either party.

176 The Child Marriage Restraint Act of 1929, also known as the Sarda Act, was a law that prohibited child marriage in India. It was passed in the Imperial Legislative Council of India on 28th September 1929 and came into effect on 1stApril, 1930.

177 The Divorce Act made it possible for both the genders to give each other a divorce, and separate.

Exemplifying and living notions of Modern-Day feminism

She, in the truest sense, embodied the essence of womanhood, feminism, and sisterhood at a time when these concepts were not widely spoken of. The Hindu philosophical concept of *Ardhanarishvara* presents a distinctive Indian understanding of gender equality and balance. This ancient wisdom provides a spiritual groundwork for feminist thought within the Indian framework. In contrast to Western feminist ideologies that often focus on confronting patriarchal systems, the *Ardhanarishvara* manifestation of Shiva and Parvati demonstrates equality as a natural, divine principle, where male and female energies exist in mutual dependence. Feminism for her meant something beyond women's empowerment in isolation and instead both masculine and feminine energies were looked at as interconnected in societal development. Within *Ardhanarishvara*, the Shakti (feminine) component embodies creativity, dynamism, and nurturing qualities, whilst the Shiva (masculine) component represents consciousness, stability, and elimination of ignorance—collectively maintaining universal equilibrium.[178] It establishes that women are not subordinate to men but instead equal participants in creation. Strict gender categorizations are questioned, and it supports an inclusive interpretation of gender, where strength and wisdom, emotion and logic, power and grace coexist naturally. The Indian feminist movement now in a lot of ways is inspired by these traditional concepts that preserve cultural and spiritual heritage. The essence

178 "Ahilyabai Holkar: A Legacy of Empowerment and Inclusivity," Chintan, October 2024, https://chintan.indiafoundation.in/articles/ahilyabai-holkar-a-legacy-of-empowerment-and-inclusivity/.

of *Ardhanarishvara*[179] was seen in Ahilyabai because of both strength and compassion in her leadership. She demonstrated a dual nature in her leadership, combining the principles of justice, administration, and military prowess akin to Shiva, whilst also displaying nurturing qualities associated with Shakti through her patronage of arts, temple construction and care for her subjects. While the modern feminist movement emphasizes the power of sisterhood and the unity and empowerment of women, she lived these principles centuries ago, offering a shining example of their transformative potential. When she was widowed, she did not become a sati because of her father-in-law's influence and insistence to not do the same and so in a way throughout her reign we see that her contribution, particularly in supporting widows and redefining gender roles, remains a testament to her commitment to the betterment of society.[180]

Womanhood and Sisterhood in Ahilya Bai's Era

During Ahilya Bai's time, the perception of womanhood was largely confined to the roles of a wife and mother.[181]

179 Ardhanarishvara is a composite deity in Hinduism that embodies both masculine and feminine principles, representing the synthesis of Shiva and Parvati (or Shakti) into a single form. The name Ardhanarishvara is derived from Sanskrit, Ardha meaning half, Nari meaning woman and Ishvara meaning Lord. This form symbolizes the ultimate unity of opposites— male and female, Purusha (cosmic consciousness) and Prakriti (creative energy), static and dynamic forces. It reflects a philosophical and spiritual understanding of gender fluidity, balance, and interconnectedness in the cosmic order. Ardhanarishvara is often depicted in iconography with one half of the body displaying Shiva's attributes (matted hair, trident, tiger skin) and the other half reflecting Parvati's characteristics (ornaments, saree, feminine grace). The deity underscores the idea that masculine and feminine energies are not separate but rather two aspects of the same divine reality, essential for creation and cosmic balance.

180 Shawrina Salam, "Ahilyabai Holkar: The Brave Maratha Queen Who Championed Women's Education and Empowerment," Feminism in India, March 1, 2022, https://feminisminindia.com/2022/03/01/ahilyabai-holkar-the-brave-maratha-queen-who-championed-womens-education-and-empowerment-indianwomeninhistory/.

181 Jahagirdhar V (2021). Karma Yogini: Life of Ahilyabai Holkar. Mehta Publishing House.

At the time the world and society functioned in a way where women were treated as mere shadows of their husbands and families and were often seen as extensions of men, their identities shaped and limited by their relationships with their husbands and families, she chose to not accept her fate. Throughout the Indian renaissance she is one of the few who decided to act when she saw the desperation in their eyes, the hopelessness that had been forced upon them. By using her resources and powers she gave these women a second chance at life and provided them with financial support, education, and training, empowering them to rebuild their lives.[182] Her initiatives extended beyond mere charitable acts, stemming from her deep-rooted conviction in women's dignity and capabilities, irrespective of whether they were married or not. Through her support for widows and her efforts to help them establish new beginnings, she transformed societal perceptions of feminine identity and mutual support, creating a legacy of women's empowerment that continues to inspire in contemporary times.

Redefining Feminism before its Time

Women's rights and anti-patriarchal movements were not explicitly defined during her time and in that period of history however, but her governance and the way she operated embodied these principles through action. In the 1760s, she fought back against societal stereotypes by engaging in traditionally male-dominated roles in governance, administration and military affairs, exemplifying early manifestations of gender equality. Her progressive outlook particularly benefited widows and she gave them resources

182 "Lokmata Ahilyabai Holkar – A Role Model for Indian Women," Organiser, November 17, 2024, https://organiser.org/2024/11/17/265723/bharat/lokmata-ahilyabai-holkar-a-role-model-for-indian-women/.

and opportunities to challenge the social stigma against widows. She dedicated specific state funds for their welfare in a society where women without male support were often seen as burdens, this was in a lot of ways a radical act of defiance against the status quo.[183]

Also, young widows in her reign were encouraged to find ways to contribute to society which included providing them with education and training, enabling them to become self-reliant and independent. She also actively intervened in the practice of sati even though she could not abolish the practice entirely, she used her influence to discourage it and to offer alternatives to women who might have felt compelled to sacrifice themselves. Her actions saved countless lives and gave women the courage to imagine a future beyond what is traditionally expected of a woman. Her leadership also extended to the younger generation of women, and she ensured young girls studied and received education.

Historical Context: Feminism in India

Devi Ahilya laid the foundation for women centric thought traditions and defined what feminism meant even before Raja Ram Mohan Roy,[184], Ishwar Chandra Vidyasagar,[185],

183 Jahagirdhar V (2021). Karma Yogini: Life of Ahilyabai Holkar. Mehta Publishing House.

184 Raja Ram Mohan Roy (1772–1833) was a pioneering Indian social reformer and the founder of the Brahmo Samaj, advocating for women's rights and progressive societal changes. His key contributions included the abolition of sati, support for widow remarriage, promotion of women's education, advocacy for women's property rights, and opposition to polygamy and child marriage.

185 Ishwar Chandra Vidyasagar (1820–1891) was a Bengali social reformer, educator, and key advocate for women's rights in India. He played a crucial role in the legalization of widow remarriage, promoted women's education, and worked to abolish child marriage.

and Savitribai Phule [186] who were the pioneers of women empowerment and started advocating for women's rights in the 19th and 20th centuries. The concept of '*Nari Shakti*' (women's power) symbolized by deities like Durga and Kali are a testament to India's deep rooted traditional ideas of what it means to be a powerful woman. However, in practice, women were often denied that sort of agency, autonomy and respect that would be seen as a key feature of these divine figures; she bridged this gap by living the ideals of *Nari shakti* in her governance and personal life. She showed how women could be both compassionate and strong, nurturing, and decisive. This duality, which is central to modern feminism that speaks of embracing femininity and doesn't just view masculine traits to be superior, was a defining feature of her leadership.

Ahilya Bai's Legacy in Modern Feminism

What we know and understand today as sisterhood is what Ahilya long back advocated for in her era, showing how she was way ahead of her time. Her advocacy for unity and solidarity amongst women are one of key founding principles of what we know of modern-day feminism. She worked towards changing various social constructs and harmful stereotypes that positioned women backwards, and her proactivity is a key takeaway for modern feminists, who continue to fight for equality and justice in various spheres of life. She redefined womanhood, feminism, and sisterhood long before these concepts became part of the global lingo

186 Savitribai Phule (1831–1897) was a pioneering social reformer, educator, and poet, widely regarded as India's first female teacher. She established the first school for girls in Pune in 1848, challenging the deeply entrenched caste and gender biases of the time. Her relentless efforts in promoting women's education laid the foundation for gender equality in India's educational system.

that we use today while explaining the very concept of feminism. Her actions challenged the oppressive norms of her time, for example, by supporting widows, inspiring others to be educated, and defying patriarchal expectations, she improved the lives of so many women and laid the groundwork for future feminist movements. In a world where women were often seen as extensions of men, she proved that they could be leaders, change-makers, and more and the principles of feminism and sisterhood that we read of today are not new; they have been embodied by women like her throughout history.

Masculine-Feminine Dichotomy: Ahilya Bai's Counter Narrative

Throughout history, the relationship between femininity, masculinity and how feminine or masculine traits affect power has been nuanced. Patriarchy has enforced its own gender-based hierarchies that position masculinity as equivalent to authority and leadership. This systematic subordination has existed because of various cultural, social, and institutional mechanisms that have perpetuated male dominance while marginalizing feminine attributes and experiences.

Dichotomy in Professional Spaces

What we see today in professional environments is the constant need for women based on internalized social constructs to adopt traditionally masculine traits to achieve recognition and success. This phenomenon is termed as "professional androgyny" by scholars like Joan Acker

(1990),[187] who explains how workspaces, institutions and other organizational structures are inherently gendered. Research by Catalyst (2007)[188] shows how women in leadership positions often face the "double-bind dilemma"- being perceived as either too feminine to be competent or too masculine to be likeable. This very pressure to masculinize behavior stems from internalized social constructs that make people feel that leadership is itself a traditionally masculine trait that requires assertiveness, competitiveness, and emotional detachment, again assumed to be or rather perceived as masculine. However, contemporary research in organizational behavior[189] such as studies by Alice Eagly and Linda Carli, show how effective leadership requires a blend of both traditionally feminine and masculine attributes-including empathy, collaboration, and relationship-building skills.

Historical Counter-Narratives: Ahilya Bai's Leadership Model

By exemplifying how her feminine attributes turned out to be a defining part of her governance she gave the exact solution which is needed for such dichotomy. Even in Tukoji Holkar's descriptions of her being "Pure as Ganges, Mother-like,"[190] she, be it inadvertently or consciously approached

187 Acker, Joan. 1990. "Hierarchies, Jobs, Bodies: A Theory of Gendered Organizations." Gender & Society 4 (2): 139–158.

188 Catalyst. 2007. The Double-Bind Dilemma for Women in Leadership: Damned If You Do, Doomed If You Don't. New York: Catalyst. https://www.catalyst.org/insights/2007/the-double-bind-dilemma-for-women-in-leadership

189 Eagly, Alice H., and Linda L. Carli. "Women and the Labyrinth of Leadership." Harvard Business Review, September 2007. https://hbr.org/2007/09/women-and-the-labyrinth-of-leadership.

190 Nagrale, N. N (1979). "AHILYABAI AND HER BENEVOLENT ADMINISTRATION." In Proceedings of the Indian History Congress, vol. 40, pp. 700-706. Indian History Congress.

leadership in a conventionally feminine way without ever having to compromise her authority or effectiveness, which is often a fear amongst women that they would not be taken seriously in the workspace if they show their compassionate side. As the ruler of Malwa in the 18th century, she exemplified how women could not only hold power but excel in governance and social reform. Her 30 -year reign (1767-1795) is celebrated for its exceptional administrative acumen, social justice, and cultural preservation.[191] Holkar's governance model demonstrates that gender is no barrier to effective leadership. She personally administered justice, managed state affairs, and led military planning, breaking contemporary stereotypes about women's capabilities in governance. Her legacy serves as a powerful historical precedent for contemporary debates about women's political representation. Ahilya Bai's reign demonstrates that when women are given opportunities for leadership, they can govern effectively and bring unique perspectives to power. Her example challenges persistent stereotypes about women's leadership capabilities and provides historical validation for current efforts to increase women's political participation globally.

As young women of the 21st Century, we often question what defines empowerment for us? Can Empowerment only be understood in economic, social, cultural or political empowerment? We often put empowerment in these compartments, restricting its meaning in the truest sense and often disconnect ourselves from the meaning of holistic empowerment which goes beyond individual empowerment but includes working for the empowerment of people

191 K. Sharma, K. ""Status and Condition of Women in the Holkar State (1734–1948)."" Proceedings of the Indian History Congress 39, no. II (1978): 801–807.

around us. Devi Ahilya all her life lived for her people, she empowered the lives of her people in the noblest way, from widow rehabilitation to inclusion of Bhil's in administrative roles. She believed true empowerment is not just fighting for rights but in just deliverance of one's duties also. Her life has laid the foundation for Indian thought tradition which has always been women centric.

Reference

1. Acker, Joan. 1990. "Hierarchies, Jobs, Bodies: A Theory of Gendered Organizations." Gender & Society 4 (2): 139–158.

2. Apte, B. K. Ahilyabai Holkar: A Study in Benevolent Administration. Pune: Sharda Publishing House, 1988.

3. Bruce, George. An Historical Sketch of the Native States of India in Subsidiary Alliance. n.d.

4. Burway, M. W. (1925). Life of His Highness Maharaja Tukoji Rao Holkar II, GCSI, Ruler of Indore (1835-1886). Holkar State Printing Press, Indore retrieved from https://archive.org/details/dli.ministry.03869/page/n9/mode/2up accessed on 17th September 2024.

5. Catalyst. 2007. The Double-Bind Dilemma for Women in Leadership: Damned If You Do, Doomed If You Don't. New York: Catalyst. https://www.catalyst.org/insights/2007/the-double-bind-dilemma-for-women-in-leadership Chakravarthy, P. Leadership Shastras: Lessons from Indian History. Westland Books, 2021.

6. Chandrasekhar, M, Yugandhara Ahilyabai Holkar: Historical Novel Focusing on The Inspiring Life of Devi Ahilya Bai Holkar, New Delhi: Prabhat Prakashan Pvt. Ltd., 2024.

7. Chopra, P. N. Queens of India. New Delhi: Diamond Pocket Books, 2004.

8. Cummings, C. 2017. "Mapping Holkar Identity." In Women,

Gender, and Art in Asia, c. 1500–1900, edited by M. B. Bose. Routledge.

9. DiMaggio, P. "Cultural Entrepreneurship in Nineteenth-Century Boston: The Creation of an Organizational Base for High Culture in America," Media, Culture & Society 4, no. 1 (1982): 33–50.

10. Divekar, V. D. "Ahilyabai Holkar and Her Economic Policies." Indian Economic and Social History Review 25, no. 3 (1988): 301-320.

11. Diwan, H. D., Sharma, A., Bhadauria, S. S., Kadwe, P., Sanyal, D., & Sharma, J. (2020). Ancient Hindu rock monuments, configuration and architectural features of Ahilya Devi Fort of Holkar Dynasty, Mahismati Region, Maheshwar, Narmada Valley, Central India. International Journal of Scientific Development and Research, 5(11), 134. Retrieved from https://www.ijsdr.org/

12. Eagly, Alice H., and Linda L. Carli. "Women and the Labyrinth of Leadership." Harvard Business Review, September 2007. https://hbr.org/2007/09/women-and-the-labyrinth-of-leadership.

13. Ellmeier, A. "Cultural Entrepreneurialism: On the Changing Relationship Between the Arts, Culture and Employment," International Journal of Cultural Policy 9, no. 1 (2003): 3–16.

14. Findly, E.B., Women, Religion, and Social Change in India (Leiden: Brill, 1985).

15. Foucault, M. Power/Knowledge: Selected Interviews and Other Writings. 1972–1977. 1980. Vintage (12 November 1980)

16. Gokhale, B. K. The Making of the Indian Nation. Bombay: Asia Publishing House, 1968.

17. Gupta, Manju. "The Architectural Contributions of Ahilyabai Holkar." Journal of Indian Art History 12 (1985): 45-58.

18. Jain, M, Vishwanath Rises and Rises: The Story of Eternal Kashi (New Delhi: Aryan Books International, 2022).

19. Joshi, Govindram Keshavram. Ahilyabai Holkar (Jivan Charitra). 1978. Hindi. Digital Library of India.

20. Kabeer, N. Inclusive Citizenship: Meanings and Expressions. London: Zed Books, 2005.

21. Kashikar, C. V. Holkar Dynasty: A Comprehensive History. Indore: Holkar Itihas Parishad, 1970.

22. Khadpekar, V, Dnyat-Adnyat: Ahilyabai Holkar (Lokavrutti), Mumbai: Rajhans Prakashan, 2024.

23. Khare, A. 2019. "Maheshwari Handloom Weaving Tradition: A Living Cultural Heritage." e-BANGI Journal 16 (7).

24. Kumar, Narendra. Lokmata Ahilyabai Holkar. Adhyayan Books, 2023.

25. Mahajan, Sumitra. Ahilyabai Holkar (unavailable in the public domain). (please mention more bibliographic details of the book).

26. Malcolm, Sir John. A Memoir of Central India: Including Malwa, and Adjoining Provinces. 1823.

27. Michael Lounsbury and Mary Ann Glynn, "Cultural Entrepreneurship: Stories, Legitimacy, and the Acquisition of Resources," Strategic Management Journal 22, no. 6–7 (2001): 545–564.

28. Mishra, R. N. Temples of India. New Delhi: Archaeological Survey of India, 1981.

29. Nagrale, N. N. 1979. "AHILYABAI AND HER

BENEVOLENT ADMINISTRATION." In Proceedings of the Indian History Congress, Vol. 40, 700-706. Indian History Congress.

30. Narayan, Jitendra. "Relevance of rājādharma of ancient India." The Indian Journal of Political Science (2004): 21

31. Nigam, M. L. Cultural History of Central India. Delhi: Sundeep Prakashan, 1980.

32. Rajput, A. 2020. "A Royal Representation of Indian Culture." International Journal of Home Science 6 (2): 375–377.

33. Ranade, Meena. Ahilyabai Holkar. 2000. Amar Chitra Katha Pvt Ltd (1 January 2000)

34. Ray, N. R. "The Status of Women in 18th Century India." Bengal Past and Present 76, no. 142 (1957): 95-110. https://archive.org/details/dli.calcutta.04050

35. Sardesai, G. S. New History of the Marathas. Bombay: Phoenix Publications, 1958.

36. Sethi, P. K., S. K. Bhatt, and R. Holkar. A Study of Holkar State Coinage. Original from the University of California and obtained from Bhatt, 1976.

37. Sharma, K. 1978. "Status and Condition of Women in the Holkar State 1734-1948." In Proceedings of the Indian History Congress, Vol. 39, 801-807. Indian History Congress.

38. Soman, S, Karma Yogini: Life of Ahilyabai Holkar (Mehta Publishing House, 2021), 56-60.

39. Swail, J., & Marlow, S. 2018. "Embrace the Masculine; Attenuate the Feminine" – Gender, Identity Work, and Entrepreneurial Legitimation in the Nascent Context. Entrepreneurship & Regional Development 30 (1–2): 256–282.

40. Thakur, V., V. n.d. Life and life's-work of Shree Devi Ahilya Bai Holkar. CiNii Research.

41. UN Women. n.d. "Leadership and Political Participation." Accessed March 4, 2025.

42. Zelliott, Eleanor. "Ahilyabai Holkar: A Magnificent Ruler, Saintly Administrator." Manushi, no. 124 (2001): 10-11.

43. Ball, Stephen J., Foucault, Power, and Education Foucault, power, and education. Routledge, 2012.

44. Rambhau (2024) Ahilyadevi, motherly queen, who ensured comprehensive development , Unheard Voices 14 MAY 2024 Year 4 | Vol. 2 accessed on https://socialstudiesfoundation.org/wp-content/uploads/2024/05/UV-14th-MAY.pdf.

45. Devidas D (2024) ,Devi Ahilyabai : More than a ruler , Unheard Voices 14 MAY 2024 | Year 4 | Vol. 2 accessed on https://socialstudiesfoundation.org/wp-content/uploads/2024/05/UV-14th-MAY.pdf.